符号中国 SIGNS OF CHINA

符号中国 SIGNS OF CHINA

古钱币

CHINESE ANCIENT CURRENCIES

"符号中国"编写组 ◎ 编著

中央民族大学出版社
China Minzu University Press

图书在版编目(CIP)数据

古钱币：汉文、英文／"符号中国"编写组编著. —北京：
中央民族大学出版社，2024.8
（符号中国）
ISBN 978-7-5660-2344-5

Ⅰ.①古… Ⅱ.①符… Ⅲ.①古钱（考古）—中国—汉、英 Ⅳ.①K875.6

中国国家版本馆CIP数据核字（2024）第016998号

符号中国：古钱币 CHINESE ANCIENT CURRENCIES

编　　著	"符号中国"编写组
策划编辑	沙　平
责任编辑	黄修义
英文指导	李瑞清
英文编辑	邱　械
美术编辑	曹　娜　郑亚超　洪　涛
出版发行	中央民族大学出版社
	北京市海淀区中关村南大街27号　　邮编：100081
	电话：（010）68472815（发行部）　传真：（010）68933757（发行部）
	（010）68932218（总编室）　　　　（010）68932447（办公室）
经销者	全国各地新华书店
印刷厂	北京兴星伟业印刷有限公司
开　本	787 mm×1092 mm　1/16　印张：12.25
字　数	170千字
版　次	2024年8月第1版　2024年8月第1次印刷
书　号	ISBN 978-7-5660-2344-5
定　价	58.00元

版权所有　侵权必究

"符号中国"丛书编委会

唐兰东　巴哈提　杨国华　孟靖朝　赵秀琴

本册编写者

方　媛

前言 Preface

中国古钱币历史悠久、源远流长，其铸造工艺独特、形制多变、种类繁多，成就了中国古代钱币蔚为大观的景象，成为东方钱币体系的代表。不同时代的钱币体系都蕴藏着当时的社会内涵，每一种钱币的文字、设计、制作、风格都是当时社会政治、经济、文化、科学技术的反映。正如中国古代流行最久的圆形方孔钱的方孔，古钱币贯穿起的中国古代各时期的历史文化，是中国古代历史文化遗存的重要方面。

本书以中国古钱币的历史发展为主线，介绍了古钱币的基础知识和流通背景：第一部分重点介绍古钱币的

Chinese ancient currencies have a long history with unique casting techniques, various shapes and abundant types, which contribute to magnificent pictures and become the representative of the oriental monetary system. The currency systems of different eras carry the social connotations of the time. Each inscription, design, production or style is the reflection of the politics, economy, culture and scientific technology. Like the circular coin (circular coin with a square hole) which prevailed in China for the longest time, the ancient currencies link the history and culture of the different periods together, which is an important aspect of Chinese ancient cultural remains.

This book takes the historical development of Chinese ancient currencies as the mainline, and introduces the basic knowledge and the

发展历史、古钱币的类型和铸造工艺；第二部分详细介绍各时代主要的钱币类型及其社会背景，有利于读者以时代为框架，详细了解中国各个时代的古钱币面貌。

background: The first section concentrates on the ancient currencies' history, types and the foundry techniques; the second section specifically introduces the currencies of different eras and their respective social backgrounds, which may be helpful for readers to understand the features of Chinese ancient currencies from different historical stages chronologically.

目录 Contents

古钱币概说
Introduction of Chinese Ancient Currencies ………… 001

中国最早的货币
The Earliest Currencies in China ………………………… 002

中国钱币的发展过程
Development of Chinese Currencies …………………… 006

古钱币的铸造工艺
Casting Techniques of Chinese Ancient
Currencies ………………………………………………… 020

古钱币的种类
Types of Chinese Ancient Currencies ………………… 029

古钱币鉴赏
Appreciation of Chinese Ancient Currencies ……… 033

先秦钱币
Currencies of the Pre-Qin Period (approx.
2070 B.C.–221 B.C.) ……………………………………… 034

秦汉钱币
Currencies of the Qin Dynasty (221 B.C.–206 B.C.)
and Han Dynasty (206 B.C.–220 A.D.) ………………… 062

三国两晋南北朝钱币
Currencies of the Three Kingdoms Period, the
Western and Eastern Jin Dynasties, and the
Southern and Northern Dynasties (220–589) ………… 079

1

隋唐钱币
Currencies of the Sui Dynasty (581–618)
and Tang Dynasty (618–907).................................. 096

五代十国钱币
Currencies of the Five Dynasties and Ten
States (907–960) 106

宋代钱币
Currencies of the Song Dynasty (960–1279) 110

辽、西夏、金代钱币
Currencies of the Liao Dynasty (907–1125),
Western Xia Dynasty (1038–1227) and
Jin Dynasty (1115–1234)... 129

元代钱币
Currencies of the Yuan Dynasty (1206–1368)....... 140

明代钱币
Currencies of the Ming Dynasty (1368–1644) 150

清代钱币
Currencies of the Qing Dynasty (1616–1911) 160

古钱币概说
Introduction of Chinese Ancient Currencies

　　钱币首先作为商品交换的手段，在人们的日常生活中有着至关重要的作用；其又常常承载着区域文化，是各国各时期政治、经济、文化、艺术的全面反映。中国古钱币伴随着中国历史文化的发展，蕴含了中国古代经济、政治、文化的方方面面，浓缩了几千年的历史进程。从最早的贝币，到先秦时期的四大钱币体系——刀币、布币、贝形钱、圜钱，再到秦始皇统一后的圆形方孔钱，以及宋代开始出现的白银和纸币等新的钱币类型，不同历史时期的钱币体系构成了中国古代钱币丰富多彩的画面。

As a method of commodity exchange currency plays a very important role in people's daily lives, and usually carries regional cultures, which can be the comprehensive reflection of the politics, economy, culture and art of each state and era. Along with the development of Chinese history and culture, Chinese ancient currencies have contained all the aspects of economy, politics and culture of the ancient China, and have concentrated the thousands of years' historical progress. From the earliest shell coin to the four coin systems of the pre-Qin Period (2070B.C.-221 B.C.)—knife-shaped coin, *Bu* coin (with a shape of spade), shell-shaped coin and round coin, and finally the circular coin (circular coin with a square hole) after the great unification by Emperor Shihuang (259B.C.-210 B.C.) of the Qin Dynasty, and the birth of the new types of currency, like the silver ingot and banknote after the Song Dynasty (960-1279), the monetary systems of different historical periods make up the rich and colorful picture of Chinese ancient currencies.

> ## 中国最早的货币

货币是商品生产和商品交换的产物。据《淮南子》记载，在上古尧帝时期就有了"以所有易所无，以所工易所拙"，"易"即交换的意思。在原始社会，为了互通有无，人们使用物物交换的方式进行贸易，牲畜、海贝、珍稀鸟类羽毛、兽皮、宝石等都曾被作为交换媒介使用。后来随着社会的发展，

- **最早的货币——海贝**
  海贝不仅可以作为交换媒介使用，还具有装饰功能。
  The Earliest Currency—Seashell
  The seashell not only can be used as the medium of exchange, but also has the function of decoration.

> ## The Earliest Currencies in China

Currency is the result of commodity production and exchange. According to the book *Huai Nan Tzu*, as early as the period of Emperor Yao in ancient China, there was an saying as "use what you get to exchange for what you need, use what you are good at to exchange what you are lack of ". In the primitive society, in order to get the needed goods, people bartered with each other. The livestock, seashell, rare bird feather, animal skin and gemstone were all used as the medium of exchange. Later, with the social development, the range of the article exchange had constantly expanded, while most of the articles used as the medium of exchange had been eliminated gradually. It wasn't until the period of the Xia Dynasty (approx. 2070

物物交换的范围不断扩大，大部分作为交换媒介的物品在贸易中逐渐被淘汰。到了夏商周时期，产于中国南方海域的海贝，因其坚固小巧、携带方便、光洁美观，很受人们的欢迎而发展成为中国最早的货币。

B.C.-1600 B.C.), Shang Dynasty (1600 B.C.-1046 B.C.) and Zhou Dynasty (1046 B.C.-256 B.C.), the seashell produced in the Southern Sea of China gained in popularity, due to its solid and small texture, portability and bright and clean appearance, became the earliest currency of China.

实物货币

实物货币是中国历史上最初的货币形式，包括珠玉、龟贝、猎器、兽皮、农具等。实物货币既有实用价值，也可作为交易媒介。在材质上，实物货币包括了金属，但并不涵盖金属货币。

Physical Currencies

The physical currencies is the initial currency type in Chinese history, including jade beads, turtle shells, hunting devices, animal skins, farm tools, etc. It not only has practical value, but also can be used as the medium of exchange. In terms of material, the commodity money includes the metal, but doesn't cover metallic currency.

• 农具四孔石铲（新石器时代）
Stone Shovel with Four Holes (Farm Tool)
(Neolithic Age, 10,000-4,000 years ago)

- 西周《三年卫盉》铭文

  铭文中有关于当时用贝交易的记载。

  Inscription on *Wei He* (a Bronze Ware) (Western Zhou Dynasty, 1046 B.C.-771 B.C.)

  The inscription recorded that people had already used shell coins for the exchanges at that time.

随着商品经济的发展和交易的扩大，海贝供不应求，用陶、石、骨、玉、铜、金、银等材料仿制的贝币大量出现。河南偃师二里头遗址曾出土有夏代的天然贝、骨贝和石贝；河南安阳殷墟

- 银贝（战国）

  Silver Seashell Coins (Warring States Period, 475B.C.-221 B.C.)

With the development of commodity economy and the expansion of trade, seashells were in short supply. Many imitative shell coins made of pottery, stone, bone, jade, bronze, gold and silver emerged. Some natural shell coins, bone coins and stone coins of the Xia Dynasty have been unearthed in Yanshi Er-li-tou site in Henan Province. In the Yin Ruins in Anyang, Henan Province, more than 1,700 pieces of seashell coins of the late Shang Dynasty were excavated from the Tomb of Fuhao.

The shell coin uses *Peng* as the computing unit. Generally speaking, the five bunched shells make "one string",

妇好墓出土有商代晚期的海贝1700余枚。

贝币以"朋"为计算单位。一般认为，五只串起来的贝为一串，两串为一朋，即一朋十贝。在中国汉字中，有不少从贝之字与财富、买卖有关，如购、赔、赏、贩、货等，可见在造字之时，人们在观念上就将"贝"与社会财富和商品交易联系在一起了。

and two strings make "one *Peng*", referred to as one *Peng* equals to ten shells. In Chinese characters, lots of them are composed by the character *Bei* (贝, seashell) with the meaning related to fortune and business, like 购 (buy), 赔 (pay for), 赏 (award), 贩 (sell), 货 (goods), etc. It's thus clear that when people made characters, they had ideally linked the *Bei* (seashell) together with the social wealth and commodity trade.

- 天然贝
Natrual Seashells

> 中国钱币的发展过程

商朝末期，随着青铜制造业的发展，出现了用青铜仿贝壳形态制成的铜贝，其出现表明了中国钱币由自然形态的货币向人工铸币的转换。在春秋战国时期，诸侯称雄割据，钱币也形成了四大体系：刀币——流通于齐、燕、赵等地；布币——流通于晋、燕等地；贝形

> Development of Chinese Currencies

In the late Shang Dynasty, with the development of the bronze manufacturing industry, people started to imitate shell coin with bronze. So the bronze coin was born, which indicates the transition of Chinese currency from the natural form to manual casting. In the Spring and Autumn Period and Warring States Period (770 B.C.-221 B.C.), the feudal aristocrats set up separate regimes, and the currency was also divided into four systems: knife-shaped coin was

- 秦始皇像

秦始皇嬴政（前259—前210），秦朝开国皇帝。他确立了方孔圆钱的钱币形制。

Portrait of Emperor Qin Shihuang

The Emperor Qin Shihuang, Ying Zheng (256 B.C.-210 B.C.), was the founding emperor of the Qin Dynasty (221 B.C.-206 B.C.). He established the shape and form of the circular coin (with a square hole).

钱——流通于楚地；圜钱——流通于秦和刀布币区。

秦始皇统一六国后，推行了一系列巩固统一，加强中央集权的政策措施，货币制度的统一为其中重要的一项。秦始皇废除了列国行用的刀币、布币等货币制度，以秦国的方孔圆钱——半两钱作为通行全国的法定货币。这一举措是中国货币史上具有划时代意义的一次重大变革，从此圆形方孔的钱币形态固定下来，在古代中国通行了两千多年。

circulated in the states of Qi, Yan, Zhao, etc.; *Bu* coin (with a shape of spade) was circulated in the states of Jin, Yan, etc.; shell-shaped coin was circulated in the state of Chu; and round coin was circulated in the state of Qin and and the circulation areas of knife-shaped coin and *Bu* coin.

After the great unification, Emperor Qin Shihuang promoted a series of policies to consolidate the situation and strengthen the central authorities. And the unification of currency regulation was an important part. The emperor abolished

方孔圆钱

方孔圆钱的形状为外圆中方，在发展过程中变化不大，仅在钱背、钱郭、钱穿、钱径、钱文书法、纹饰等细节方面有所不同。古钱币的造型多样，即使同一钱形，也有大小、轻重、成分、质料、版别、面文、背文、钱穿、内郭、外郭等差异。

方孔圆钱总体上可以分为铢两钱阶段和宝文钱阶段。秦至唐武德四年（621年）前，钱币的名称都是以重量单位铢、两为名；唐武德四年开始铸"开元通宝"钱，从此钱币不再以铢、两为名，而是以"宝"为名，这种命名方式一直延续到清末，并影响了日本、朝鲜、越南等周边国家。

Circular Coin (Circular Coin with a Square Hole)

The circular coin with round shape and a square hole in the middle didn't change much during its development. It only has some differences on the back, *Guo* (rim), *Chuan* (hole), diameter, calligraphy of the inscription, motif, etc. The form of ancient coins varied. Even with the same shape, coins still differ on the size, weight, composition, texture, edition, facial inscription, back inscription, *Chuan*, inner *Guo*, outer *Guo*, etc.

The development of circular coin generally can be divided into two phases: *Zhu-Liang* coin stage and *Bao-Wen* coin stage. From the Qin Dynasty to the fourth year of Wude Period of the Tang Dynasty (221 B.C.-621 A.D.), coin was named after its weight unit: *Zhu* and *Liang*; from the year 621, the government started to cast *Kaiyuan Tongbao* coin. Thence, coin was named after *Bao* instead of *Zhu* and *Liang*. This naming method was passed down to the end of the Qing Dynasty (1616-1911) and greatly influenced the neighboring countries like Japan, Korea, Vietnam, etc.

- **康熙通宝**

面，指钱币的正面，其背面则称"背"。穿，指钱币的穿孔，也称"好"。郭，指钱币的边缘、穿孔四周凸起的部分，其中钱币外缘称"外郭"，穿孔四周的称"内郭"。钱文，指钱币上的文字、图案和符号等。肉，指钱币除钱文、内外郭以外的钱体的表面部分，也指钱体的厚薄程度。边道，指钱币边缘的侧面部分。

Kangxi Tongbao

Face, indicates the front side of the coin, and its back side is called as "back"; *Chuan*, indicates the hole in the middle of the coin, also called as *Hao*; *Guo*, indicates the rim of the coin and the bulging part around the hole. And the outer rim of the coin is called as outer *Guo*, while the bulging part around the hole is called as inner *Guo*; inscription, indicates the characters, patterns and motifs carved on the coin; *Rou* (flesh), indicates the rest exterior part of the coin body except for the inscription, inner and outer rim, which also refers to the thickness of the coin body; side path, indicates the side part of the coin rim.

汉初承袭秦制，继续铸行半两钱。此外，汉高祖推行"无为"政治，允许民间私铸钱，民间铸钱轻如"榆荚"，俗称"榆荚钱"。因导致通货膨胀，民间铸钱被禁止。汉武帝时期，统一全国铜币铸造权，建立了

the currency regulations of other states like knife-shaped coin, spade-money, etc., and made the circular coin (*Ban-Liang* coin, circular coin with a square hole) as the legal currency of the nation. This measure was an epoch-making revolution in the history of Chinese currency.

五铢钱制度。五铢钱一直沿用到唐初，成为中国钱币史上使用时间最长的一种钱币。

- **汉武帝像**

汉武帝刘彻（前156—前87），汉朝的第七位皇帝。他雄才大略、文治武功，在位期间使西汉王朝达到了最繁荣鼎盛的时期。

Portrait of Emperor Wu of the Han Dynasty

The Emperor Wu of the Han Dynasty, Liu Che (156B.C.-87B.C.), was the seventh emperor of the Han Dynasty. With great talent and outstanding political and military achievements, he made the Western Han Dynasty reach its most prosperous and flourishing era.

Since then, the form of circular coin was adopted and circulated in ancient China for more than two thousand years.

In the early Han Dynasty (206 B.C.-25 A.D.), the government followed the regulation of the Qin Dynasty and continuously founded *Ban-Liang* coin. Besides, the emperor Gaozu carried out the "Inactivity" politics, allowing the civil workshop to cast money privately. The coin was as light as elms' seed, commonly called as "elms-seed coin", which led to the inflation and finally was banned by the government. In the reign of Emperor Wu of the Han Dynasty, the authority unified the bronze coin's foundry right throughout the nation and established the *Wu-Zhu* coin system which was circulated until the early Tang Dynasty (618-907), becoming the coin of longest lifetime in the Chinese currency history.

- **五铢钱（汉）**

从汉武帝开始铸造的五铢钱是中国钱币史上流通最久、铸造数量最多的钱币。

***Wu-Zhu* Coin (Han Dynasty, 206 B.C.-220 A.D.)**

The *Wu-Zhu* coin cast from the reign of Emperor Wu of the Han Dynasty was the coin of the longest lifetime and the largest quantity in the Chinese currency history.

东西汉之交、王莽称帝时期，一共进行了四次货币改革，使货币制度极度混乱，流通的货币有错刀、货布、货泉、小泉五十、小泉十一、大布黄千等。

东汉初，经济基础薄弱，社会动荡，币值混乱，半两钱、五铢钱、新莽货币混杂流通。到建武十六年（40年），汉光武帝刘秀下令复铸五铢钱，即建武五铢。到汉桓帝之后，通货膨胀严重，开始流行"磨边五铢""剪边五铢"和"綖环五铢"，这些货币不是法定货币，是私铸者

In the interim of the Western Han Dynasty and Eastern Han Dynasty (the period of Wang Mang, 9-25), there were four monetary reforms being carried out, which made the monetary system trap in chaos. The circulating currencies included *Cuo-Dao* coin (of knife-shape), *Huo-Bu* coin, *Huo-Quan* coin, *Xiaoquan Wushi* (fifty), *Xiaoquan Shiyi* (eleven), *Dabu Huangqian*, etc.

In the early Eastern Han Dynasty, facing the situation of the weak economic foundation, social turmoil currency chaos and the disordered circulation of *Ban-Liang* coin, *Wu-Zhu* coin and the *Xinmang* coins, Emperor Guangwu, Liu Xiu ordered to recast the *Wu-Zhu* coin, which was the *Jianwu Wu-Zhu* coin in the 16th year of the Jianwu Period (40). By Emperor Huan, inflation got serious. The illegal currencies like edging *Wu-Zhu* coin, sheering *Wu-Zhu* coin and *Yanhuan Wu-Zhu* coin were circulated in the market. Those privately cast coins directly caused the economic chaos,

- 铜人俑（东汉）
董卓将铜材制作的人俑熔铸，制成无文小钱。
Copper Statue (Eastern Han Dynasty, 25-220)
Dong Zhuo used the copper statues to found copper coins.

谋取私利所铸，直接导致了经济混乱、物价昂贵，人民生活贫困。中平三年（186年），汉灵帝改铸"四出五铢"，从方孔的四角各模铸一道阳文直线抵达外郭，用来区别旧钱。献帝初平年间，董卓攻入长安，取铜人、铜台等熔铸无文小钱，这是东汉最后一次铸钱。

三国两晋南北朝时期长期处于分裂状态，货币体制混乱，钱币流通不畅，形制大小不一，劣钱泛滥。三国两晋包含魏、蜀、吴三国鼎立和两晋、十六国两个历史时期。三国时期，各国在沿用汉代旧钱的基础上，各个政权自铸钱币，颁行币制；两晋时期，主要沿用汉魏五铢钱和孙吴旧钱，兼用谷帛等实物，没有铸新钱；西晋末年，历经五胡十六国，各割据政权多自行铸造区域性的地方钱币，在钱文中出现年号、国号、吉语等，打破了传统的铢两之称。

东晋沿用吴地旧钱，大小轻重不一。"大泉五百""大泉当千"的大钱，谓之"比轮"；中等大小的钱又叫"四文"，即五铢钱，可当四枚小钱使用；吴兴（今浙

rising price, which made people live in poverty and misery. In 186, Emperor Ling cast the *Sichu Wu-Zhu* coin, with four straight lines cast in relief at each corner of the square hole to the outer rim to differentiate from the old coin. From 190 to 193, Dong Zhuo invaded into Chang'an and used the copper statues and copper platforms to cast copper coins, which was the last coin-foundry in the Eastern Han Dynasty.

During the period of the Three Kingdoms Period, the Western and Eastern Jin dynasties, and the Southern and Northern dynasties (220-589), China was in divided situation for a long time; the monetary system was in chaos; currency circulation was not smooth; shapes and forms of coins were not unified; inferior money over owed. This period includes two historical stages: the tripartite confrontation of Wei, Shu, Wu (three states) and the confrontation between the Jin (Western Jin and Eastern Jin) and Sixteen States (successive northern feudalistic authorities). In the former stage, not only following the old currency form of Han Dynasty, the three states also cast their own coins and issued their own monetary regulations. In the later stage, they mainly adopted the

江湖州市内）沈充所铸五铢小钱，轻薄小巧，称为"沈郎钱"，以"文"为计量单位。

东晋之后，公元420—589年，南方地区经历了宋、齐、梁、陈四朝，史称南朝，南朝各朝皆铸有钱币。

从公元386年北魏建国到公元581年隋朝统一北方，北方先后经历了北魏、东魏、西魏、北齐、北周几个政权时期，史称北朝。北朝多用谷帛交易，铸币不多。西魏恭帝三年（556年），宇文泰之子宇文觉废拓跋廓称帝，改国号为"周"，史称北周。北周模仿王莽币制，铸造的钱币有"布泉""五行大布""永通万国"，俗称"北周三钱"。

公元581年，隋朝建立，结束了三国两晋南北朝以来长期分裂割据的局面。战乱之余，钱币制度紊乱。隋初，北方仍然流行旧钱，不久隋文帝下令整顿货币，禁止旧钱流通，铸造五铢钱，使货币制度得到统一。

到了唐代，钱制进入一个新的时代，"开元通宝"的铸行，结束

Wu-Zhu coin of Han-Wei (the kingdom of Wei) and the old coin of Sun-Wu (the Kingdom of Wu), as well as the commodity money like grain and silk, and didn't cast new money. At the end of the Western Jin Dynasty (265-317), each separated state founded its own regional coins with inscriptions of reign titles, dynasty titles, auspicious words, etc., which broke the *Zhu-Liang* tradition.

In the Eastern Jin Dynasty (317-420), they followed the old coin of Wu, with various sizes and weights. The large coins like *Daquan Wubai* (five hundred) and *Daquan Dangqian* (one thousand) were called as *Bilun*; the middle coins were called as *Siwen*, also known as *Wu-Zhu* coin, which could be used as four little coins; the *Wu-Zhu* little coin cast by Shen Chong of Wuxing (in today's Huzhou City, Zhejiang Province), was small and exquisite, also known as Shen's coin, using *Wen* as the unit.

After the Eastern Jin Dynasty, from 420 to 589, the southern area was ruled by Song, Qi, Liang, Chen, four regimes successively, which was called as the Southern dynasties. Each regime had its own coin.

From the founding of Northern Wei in 386 to the unification of the north

● 唐高祖像

唐高祖李渊(566-635)，唐朝开国皇帝。

Portrait of Emperor Gaozu of the the Tang Dynasty

The Emperor Gaozu of the Tang Dynasty, Li Yuan (566-635), was the founding emperor of Tang.

了自秦代以来以重量命名的钱币体系，实行以"文"为货币单位的宝文钱制，揭开了中国钱币史的新篇章。唐代时，金银铸币也开始进入流通。唐中期还出现了类似汇票性质的飞钱。

五代十国是唐末藩镇割据的延续。五代，是指中原地区从朱温建立后梁起，接连更替的五个朝代，分别是后梁、后唐、后晋、后汉、

by Sui in 581, the northern area was governed by Northern Wei, Eastern Wei, Western Wei, Northern Qi, Northern Zhou, five regimes, which was called as the Northern dynasties. They mostly traded by grain and silk and barely cast coins. In 556, Yuwen Jue dethroned Tuoba Kuo and became the king. He changed the dynasty title into "Zhou", also known as the Northern Zhou in the history. They imitated the currency system of Wang Mang, and cast the coins like *Buquan*, *Wuxing Dabu*, and *Yongtong Wanguo*, commonly called as "Three Coins of the Northern Zhou".

In 581, the Sui Dynasty was established, which ended the long-term divided situation during the Three Kingdoms Period, the Western and Eastern Jin dynasties, and the Southern and Northern dynasties (220-589). Except the turmoil caused by war, the monetary system was also in chaos. In the early Sui Dynasty, the old coin was still circulated in the northern area. Soon, Emperor Wen of the Sui Dynasty ordered to reorganize the currency, banned the use of old coin, and cast *Wu-Zhu* coin, which made the monetary system unified.

In the Tang Dynasty (618-907), the currency system entered a new era. The

后周五个政权；十国是指在五代时期与中原政权对应的割据国家，分别是吴、前蜀、吴越、楚、闽、南汉、荆南、后蜀、南唐、北汉十个地方割据政权。

五代十国时期，政局十分动荡，币制也较为混乱。这一时期由于铜材匮乏，各割据政权便用铁、锡、铅、合金铁等材料铸造钱币，

- **后周世宗像**
  后周世宗柴荣（921—959），五代时期后周皇帝。
  The Emperor Shizong of the Later Zhou of the Five Dynasties
  Chai Rong (921-959), was the emperor of Later Zhou in the Five Dynasties.

foundry and circulation of "*Kaiyuan Tongbao*" ended the weight-naming system passed down ever since the Qin Dynasty, and carried out the *Bao-Wen* system by using *Wen* as measure unit, which ushered in a new page in the Chinese currency history. In this period, the gold and silver coins also appeared in the circulation field. In the middle stage of the Tang Dynasty, the *Feiqian* with the similar feature of exchange bill stepped into the stage of history.

The Five dynasties and Ten states (907-960) period was the continuance of the separation of local military government at the end of the Tang Dynasty. The Five dynasties means the five successive dynasties since Zhu Wen founded the authority Later Liang in the Central Plains, which are Later Liang, Later Tang, Later Jin, Later Han, Later Zhou. The Ten states means ten local military authorities which confronted the regimes in the Central Plains in the same period, including Wu, Former Shu, Wu Yue, Chu, Min, Southern Han, South of Jing, Later Shu, Southern Tang and Northern Han.

In the Five dynasties and Ten states, the political situation was in turmoil, and so was the currency system. Due to

• 陕西渭南华县发现的宋代钱窖 (图片提供: CFP)
Coin Cellar of the Song Dynasty in Huaxian County of Weinan City, Shaanxi Province

the shortage of copper, each local government used materials like iron, tin, led, alloy to cast coin which was of low quality.

Chinese coin foundry reached its peak in the Song Dynasty (960-1279). Under the unified central authority, the coin-casting tended to be in standard: Firstly, the name of the coin was determined uniformly by the government. The reign title of the Song Dynasty was changed frequently. Each emperor had his own one. And most coins were named after the reign title, also known as the reign title coin, which was passed down by the descendants. Secondly, the coin of Song Dynasty varied in different values, including *Zhe Er* (two), *Zhe San* (three), *Zhe Wu* (five), *Dang Shi* (ten), etc., which met the demands of circulation. Then referring to the material, the authority adopted the policy of both using copper and iron. Besides, the paper money emerged as the credit currency

质量低劣。

　　中国钱币铸造在宋代达到鼎盛。在统一的中央集权统治之下，钱币铸造趋于规范。首先，钱币的名称由朝廷统一确定。宋代年号更迭频繁，每个皇帝更换一个年号，钱币的名称多含年号，即年号钱，这一命名方式为后代相承。其次，宋代钱币有不同的当值，出现了折

二、折三、折五、当十等钱，适应了市场流通的需要。再次，在币材上，宋代采取铜铁并用的政策，不同的区域流通不同的钱币，出现了铜钱区、铁钱区和铜铁钱兼行区等。此外，作为信用货币的纸币开始出现，并得以广泛应用。宋钱钱文书法颇为讲究，北宋钱文有楷、草、行、篆、隶五体，同一种书体也有不同的风格，大多铸成对钱，到南宋时钱文则逐步趋向同一。

北宋初年，四川成都地区商业繁荣，通行的货币是铁钱。由于铁钱分量重，价值低，使用极为不便，于是出现了具有信用兑换的票据——"交子"。"交"是交换凭据，合券取钱的意思。"子"是四川方言的尾音。交子是中国也是世界上最早出现和流行的纸币，在货币史、印刷史、版画史上都占有重要的地位。

唐末至五代时期，辽、西夏、金等政权多沿用唐宋旧钱，自铸币较少。

明清时期基本上是银、钱并用的时代，银、钱比价波动很大。明朝中期因推行宝钞有几个年号很少

and was used widely. The inscription calligraphy of the money was paid lots of attention to the details, including five fonts as *Kai, Cao, Xing, Zhuan, Li*. Even the same font had different styles. The coin was mostly cast in pair. By the Southern Song Dynasty (1127-1279), the inscription trended towards unification.

In the early Northern Song Dynasty, the business was blooming in Chengdu district, Sichuan Province. The circulation currency was iron coin. Owing to its heavy weight and low value, it was not convenient for trading. Consequently, *Jiaozi* the bill for the credit exchange was born. *Jiao* means the exchange receipt; when people needed to withdraw the money, they just combined the receipts together. *Zi* is the ending syllable of Sichuan dialect. *Jiaozi* is the earliest circulated paper currency not only in China but also throughout the world, which has an important position in the currency history, printing history and print-picture history.

In the period from the late Tang Dynasty to the Five dynasties, the authorities raised in the north, like Liao, Western Xia, Jin, etc., which confronted with the Northern Song and Southern Song regimes for ages. They mostly

铸钱，而清朝历代皇帝都新铸年号钱。清朝末期，中国的人工浇铸钱币工艺受到冲击，出现了机制货币，银元、铜元、银行纸币相继被广泛使用，方孔圆钱逐渐退出历史舞台。

• 机制币 (图片提供：全景正片)
Manufactured Coins

followed the old money system of the Tang Dynasty and the Song Dynasty barely cast their own coins.

In the period of the Ming Dynasty (1368-1644) and Qing Dynasty (1616-1911), silver ingot and coin were used at the same time. The exchange rate of silver and coin fluctuated a lot. In the middle period of the Ming Dynasty, due to the implementation of treasure bill, the governments barely cast coin in several reigns. And the authorities of the Qing Dynasty used their own reign titles to cast coins. In the late Qing Dynasty, the technique of manual coin-casting was stricken in China. The manufactured coin, silver ingot, copper ingot, and paper note emerged and were widely used. The circular coin (with a square hole) gradually vanished from the stage of history.

古钱币的别称

古钱币除了拥有特定的名称外，还有许多别称，如泉、王老、腰缠、青蚨、阿堵物和孔方兄等。

泉：因钱与"泉"谐音，战国时期称钱为"泉"。《周礼·地官·泉府》贾公颜疏："泉与钱，今古异名。"泉泛指方孔圆钱，寓以"周流四方"的意义。古代掌管收购市面上滞销物及借贷息的机构叫泉府。中国现存最早的古钱专著是南宋洪遵撰写的《泉志》。今天的钱学家也称作泉学家。

王老：唐玄宗时通用的钱币上铸有"元宝"二字，当时有个富商叫王元宝，被人们所尊敬、仰慕，于是钱币就被称作"王老"。

腰缠：古人常把钱币放在腰带里，再把腰带缠绕腰间。"腰缠"也就发展成为人们对随身携带钱币的一个别称。成语"腰缠万贯"就形容那些资财富足的人。

青蚨：《淮南子》载有青蚨还钱的传说。青蚨是南方的一种虫，形状似蝉、蝶。这种虫类产卵时必须依附于花草的叶子上，但是不管别人怎么挪弄或藏起它的卵，母青蚨都能将卵找出。有人根据青蚨的这一特点，将母青蚨的血涂在81枚铜钱上，将子青蚨的血涂在另外81枚铜钱上，每次出去买东西，有时用母钱，有时用子钱，用掉的钱都会再飞回来，这样循环往复，钱就永远都用不完了。商家常将"青蚨归来"作为吉利语，寓意钱会"飞"来。

阿堵物：西晋大臣王衍崇尚清谈，从不言钱。有一次在他熟睡时，他的妻子叫仆人绕着床边堆起一大圈钱。王衍醒来，无法下床，便呼叫仆人"快拿开阿堵物"。"阿堵物"便成为钱的别称。

孔方兄：西晋文学家鲁褒在《钱神论》中描述钱币时说"亲之如兄，字曰孔方"，对钱称兄道弟。后来，孔方兄就泛指货币和财富。

Alternative Names of Ancient Coins

Except for their particular names, ancient coins have many alternative names, like: *Quan*, *Wanglao*, *Yaochan*, *Qingfu*, *A-Du Wu*, *Kong-Fang Xiong*, etc.

Quan: Due to its homophonic pronunciation with money (*Qian*), money was also called as *Quan* in the Warring States Period (475 B.C.-221 B.C.). According to *Rites of Zhou, Diguan, Mansion of Quan*, Jia Gongyan said: "*Quan* and *Qian* are synonyms." *Quan* generally refers to the circular coin (with a square hole), with the meaning of circulating around the world. In ancient time, the institution responsible for purchasing the unsalable and the credit business was called mansion of *Quan*. The earliest monograph about ancient currency, *Records of Quan*, was written by Hong Zun in the Southern Song Dynasty. Today's currency scholar is also called *Quan* scholar.

Wanglao: The coin circulated in the reign of Emperor Xuanzong of the Tang Dynasty was cast with two characters of *Yuan Bao*. At that time, there was a rich merchant named Wang Yuanbao, who was worshiped and admired by people. So the coin was called as *Wang Lao*.

Yaochan: The ancients often put the coins in the waistband, and then bound it around the waist. *Yaochan* was developed as an alias for the carry-on coins. The idiom *Yaochan Wanguan* describes the people of huge fortune.

Qingfu: According to *Huai Nan Tzu*, there was a legend about *Qingfu* paying back the money: *Qingfu* is a kind of insect in the southern area, with the appearance like cicada and butterfuly. It lays the eggs on the leaves. And no matter how you move or hide its eggs, the mother *Qingfu* will find out. Due to this characteristic, someone smeared the mother *Qingfu*'s blood on 81 coins and the baby *Qingfu*'s blood on another 81 coins. Everytime he went out and bought things, he sometimes used the mother coin and sometimes used the baby coin. Those spent coins would fly back again and again. In this way, money would never be used out. The business man often considered the words "*Qingfu Guilai*" as an auspicious blessing, meaning the money will fly back.

A-Du Wu: The minister of the Western Jin, Wang Yan, barely cared for the fame or wealth, and never talked about money. One time, when he was in deep sleep, his wife ordered the servant to pile up heaps of money around his bed. When he woke up and couldn't get out of bed, so he asked the servant to move away those *A-Du Wu*. Later, *A-Du Wu* became the alias of money.

Kong-Fang Xiong: The literati of the Western Jin, Lu Bao once described money in *Theory of the Money God*, "as close as brother (*Xiong* in Chinese), called as *Kong Fang*", and regarded the money as brother. Later, *Kong-Fang Xiong* generally indicated coins and wealth.

• 古钱币
Ancient Coins

> 古钱币的铸造工艺

中国的古钱币除了实物货币和纸币，其他货币都是用金属铸造的。古钱币的铸造工艺历史悠久，采用的是冶铸法，包括范铸法和翻砂法两种铸造工艺。直到清朝末期，随着国外机制生产工艺的引进，采用机器制造钱币的方法才大为推广。

范铸法

范铸法采用钱范铸钱的方法，

> Casting Techniques of Chinese Ancient Currencies

Except for the physical currency and paper money, Chinese ancient currencies were mostly cast by metals. The coin-casting technique has a long history, including model-casting method and sand-copy-casting method. By the late Qing Dynasty, with the introduction of the foreign machining production technique, the method of using machine to found coins was widely promoted.

Model-casting Method

The model-casting method applies the coin model to found money, which was used in the early stage of coin-casting in China. The specific procedure is: Firstly,

- "赵"字布币钱范（春秋战国）
  Coin Model of the *Bu* Coin with Character *Zhao* (Spring and Autumn Period and Warring States Period, 770 B.C.-221 B.C.)

是中国早期铸币采用的铸造方法。具体工艺是先制范，泥陶范需要在烘范窑里烘烤，用熔炉加热熔化金属，浇铸金属溶液入范内，等溶液冷却后，取出铸币，然后用一根方形铁条穿入钱穿，打磨钱边缘上的毛刺，铸币才算完成。

the clay model needs to be fired in the kiln. And melt down the metal by being heated in the smelter; pour the metallic solution into the model. After the solution is cooling, take out the coin and drive an iron bar of square intersecting surface through it to make a square hole in the middle. Then polish the burrs at the edge of the coin. So the coin is completed.

钱范

钱范是古代铸钱工艺中所使用的范和模的统称。模是制范的工具，模中的钱文为阳文正书。范直接用于铸钱，在其型腔内浇灌金属液体，即可浇铸成钱币，范内钱文为阴文反书。钱范的好坏直接影响到钱币的铸造质量。

依据功能不同，钱范可分为子范、母范、祖范与钱样范。

子范是用来浇铸钱币的钱范。早期的子范型腔是人工刻制出来的，后来发展出印制和用模型翻刻的品种。

母范是用来翻制子范的模具，多是用模具翻制而成，也有少数印制的。

祖范是用来翻制母范的模具，上有人工刻印的型腔。

钱样范是用来印制泥陶母范的凸体模型所用的模具。钱样范由祖范翻制而成，范体上有1—2枚待铸钱币的型腔，印出的钱型较统一。

依据制作材料的不同，可分为泥陶范、石范、铜范。

Coin Model

The coin model is the general term of the *Fan* and *Mu* used in the coin-casting. *Mu* is the tool to make *Fan*. The inscription in the *Mu* is carved in relief regularly. The *Fan* is used to cast money directly. Pour the metallic solution into its cavity and found the coins. The inscription in the *Fan* is carved in intaglio reversely. The quality of the coin model will affect the coins directly.

According to different functions, coin models can be divided into son-model, mother-model, ancestor-model and sample-model.

Son-model was used to cast coins. The early model cavity was carved manually. And later, the printing and model-copying types developed.

Mother-model was used to copy the son-model. It was mostly made by model-copying; rare was printed.

Ancestor-model was used to copy the mother-model with manually carved cavity.

Sample-model was used to print the convex model of the clay mother-model, and it was copied by the ancestor-model. There are one or two coins' shape cavities on the model body. The shape of the coins made by this model is unified.

According to the different materials, coin model can be divided into clay-model, stone-model, and copper-model.

• 元凤五铢陶范（西汉）

泥陶范主要是用可塑性强的黏土制成。泥陶范在使用时，要在范面涂上一层用泥炭、石英粉等混合成的涂料，以方便脱模和提高范体的耐高温性能。泥陶范一范铸一钱，春秋战国时期铸造布币和刀币的泥陶范是现存最早的泥陶范。

Clay-model of *Wu-Zhu* in Yuanfeng Period (Western Han Dynasty, 206 B.C.-25 A.D.)

The clay-model was made by the the clay with high plasticity. While using it, people should paint a layer of coating made from peat and silica flour to let the coins easily peeled off from the model and raise the model's anti-high temperature behavior. In the Spring and Autumn Period and Warring States Period (770 B.C.-221 B.C.), the clay-models of the *Bu* coin and knife-shaped coin are the earliest exsiting models.

• 布泉铜范（新莽时期）

铜范的材料是青铜，光滑清洁，能反复使用，使铸钱的效率大大提高。使用铜范前，最好在范面涂上一层涂料，既调节了铸钱的冷却时间，又降低了高温金属溶液对铜范的损伤程度，延长了铜范的使用寿命。先秦时期，铜范仅用来铸齐刀和蚁鼻钱。战国时期楚国制造的铜贝模是中国现存最大的铜钱模。

Copper-model of *Buquan* (Xinmang Period, 9-23)

The copper-model is made from bronze, sleek and clean, and can be used repeatedly, which makes the efficiency raise a lot. Before using the copper-model, a layer of coating should be painted which can modify the cooling time of the casting-coins and also can lighten the abrasion from the high-temperatured metallic solution and extend its service life. In the pre-Qin period (approx. 2070 B.C.-221 B.C.), the copper-model was only used to cast knife-shaped coin of Qi and the *Yibi* coin. During the Warring States Period (475 B.C.-221 B.C.), the copper-model of shell coin made by the state Chu is the largest exsiting copper-model in China.

- **三铢石范（西汉）**

  石范主要是由质地细腻、适于雕刻、耐高温的灰绿色软石，以及青石板和石膏制成。和泥陶范一样，石范在使用前，也要在范面涂上一层涂料。早期石范通常是一范铸两钱，后来发展成一范铸3—5枚钱。

  Stone-model of *San-Zhu* (Western Han Dynasty, 206 B.C.-25 A.D.)

  The stone-model is mainly made of the grayish-green soft stone of fine and smooth texture and anti-high temperature behavior which is suitable for carving, as well as blue slabstone and plaster. Similar to the clay-model, before using, it should be painted by a layer of coating. The early stone-model can cast two coins within one model and then three or five coins in one model.

范铸法铸钱分为阴文子范法和阳文母范法。阴文子范法又分为泥陶原范法、石雕原范法和铜铸原范法。

泥陶原范法是东周时期的一种铸钱方法，先用细黏土制成所需钱范的外形，再刻出钱的阴文形状和文字，留出浇道，烘干后，便可铸钱。泥陶原范法的缺点是一范一钱，需要毁范取钱。

石雕原范法是在石范上雕刻出多个阴文钱形，在一端留有浇口、浇道，直接浇铸铜液，取出铸钱，

The model-casting methods can be divided into concave son-model method and convex mother-model method. The former one includes: clay-model method, stone-model method and copper-model method.

Clay-model method was used in the Eastern Zhou Dynasty (770 B.C.-256 B.C.). Firstly, build the external form of the coin model by clay and carve out the shape of the coin and inscriptions in intaglio, leave the pouring gate, after drying, it can be used to found coins. The shortcoming of this method is that one

加工后，才可作为流通用的钱币。石雕原范法的钱范可多次使用，而且一次铸钱的数量较多。

铜铸原范法需要铸造铜质钱范，铸造原理与石雕原范法相同，且钱范更加坚固，可反复使用，大大提高了铸钱效率。

阳文母范法是出现在西汉以后的一种更为先进的铸钱方法。先制造出不同质地的阳文母范，再用阳文母范去制作多个阴文子范，将母范和子范叠合在一起，统一浇铸，取出铸钱后，再逐个打磨。阳文母范法的钱范不用接触高温，且经久耐用，因此一直流行到翻砂铸钱法问世。

model only can cast one coin. And the model must be destroyed in order to take out the coin.

Stone-model method is to carve out several coin shapes in intaglio and leave the pouring gate at one end and then, directly pour in the copper solution, take out the coins, after processing, the coin can finally be used in the market. The stone-model can be used repeatedly and can cast many coins at one time.

Copper-model method needs to cast the copper model. The principle is same as the stone-model method. And the model itself is more solid and can be used repeatedly, which raised the efficiency a lot.

The convex mother-model method emerged after the Western Han Dynasty (206 B.C.-25 A.D.), and is a more advanced technique. Firstly, make out the convex mother-models of different textures, and use them to produce several concave son-models, overlap the two types of models together and cast coins one by one, after taking out the coins, then polish them thoroughly. By this method, the model doesn't need to access to the high temperature and is more durable. So it prevailed until the birth of sand-copy-casting method.

• 无边五铢阳文铜制范盒（南北朝）
Convex Copper Model Case of Rimless *Wu-Zhu* (Southern and Northern Dynasties, 420-589)

钱文

钱文是指铸在或刻在钱币上的文字、符号、纹饰。钱币正面的钱文称"面文",背面的钱文称"背文"或"幕文"。中国钱币中最早出现的钱文是战国时期楚国的郢爰金版,正面钤印"郢爰"二字的阴文印记。

钱文的书写顺序与古人的书写习惯基本一致,但也有一些特殊的书写顺序,所以钱文有各种读法。常见的有顺读、旋读、横读三种读法。顺读是按照自上而下、自右到左顺序阅读钱文,是最常见的钱文读法;旋读是指从上按顺时针方向阅读钱文,是宋代最为多见的钱文读法;横读是按照先左后右或先右后左的顺序阅读钱文。

Inscription

Inscription means the characters, signs and motifs cast and carved on the coins. The inscription on the front side of a coin is called "face inscription"; and those on the back is called "back inscription" and "screen inscription". The earliest coin inscription in China is the gold coin in the state Chu in Warring States Period (475B.C.-221 B.C.). Its front carved with *Ying* and *Yuan* two characters in intaglio.

The order of the inscription is consistent with ancients' writing habit. But there are some special orders too. So the inscriptions have various ways of reading. The common ones are regular, revolving, and horizontal reading methods. The regular is based on the order of from the top

- **乾元重宝(唐)**

钱文为顺读,自上而下再自右到左为"乾元重宝"四个字。

Qianyuan Zhongbao (Tang Dynasty, 618-907)

It should be read in regular order, from the top to bottom and then from the right to the left, which is *Qian*, *Yuan*, *Zhong* and *Bao*, four characters.

- **嘉定元宝(南宋)**

钱文为旋读,自上按顺时针方向为"嘉定元宝"四个字。

Jiading Ingot (Southern Song Dynasty, 1127-1279)

It should be read in revolving order, in the clockwise direction, which is *Jia Ding Yuan Bao*, four characters.

to the bottom and then from the right to the left, which is the most common reading method; the revolving is in clockwise direction from the top part, which is the most common way in the Song Dynasty (960-1279); the horizontal is based on the order of from the left to the right or from the right to the left.

- 半两钱（秦）

钱文为横读，自右到左为"半两"二字。

Ban-Liang Coin (Qin Dynasty, 221B.C.-206 B.C.)

It should be read in horizontal order, from the right to the left, which is *Ban Liang*, two characters.

翻砂法

翻砂法铸钱出现在唐代前后，到宋代工艺已非常成熟，并一直沿用到机制法铸钱的出现为止。始铸于唐武德四年的"开元通宝"钱，制作精良，是母钱翻砂法铸钱的样板钱。翻砂法铸钱大大提高了钱币的铸造量，是钱币铸造工艺的一大进步。

Sand-copy-casting Method

The sand-copy-casting method emerged around the Tang Dynasty (618-907). By the Song Dynasty (960-1279), the technique was already matured and was adopted until the introduction of machining coin-casting. The *Kaiyuan Tongbao* coin was cast firstly in the 4th year of Wude Period of Tang Dynasty, which was finely produced and was the sample coin of the sand-copy-casting. This method greatly raised the casting quantity of the coins, and was a great progress in coin-casting technique.

- **《天工开物·铸钱图》宋应星（明）**

明代宋应星在《天工开物》中详细记载和描述了母钱翻砂法的工艺过程：用四根长一尺一寸、宽一寸二分的木条围成空框，作为铸钱模，框中填实极细的土炭末。上面微撒杉木炭灰或柳木炭灰，或用松香与清油熏模。然后将百文母钱置于上面，再用同样的方法填实一框，合盖在上面，成为钱的背框。覆转两框，则母钱落在后框上。又用一框填实，合上后框，转覆。这样合成数十框，用绳捆紧固定，将熔化的铜液灌注在木框上弦留出的铜眼孔中。待冷却后，开框，则出现树枝状的钱。将钱夹出逐一摘断，磨锉加工，便制作出一枚枚的铜钱。

Picture of Money-Casting in Exploitation of the Works of Nature by Song Yingxing (Ming Dynasty, 1368-1644)

The famous scholar of the Ming Dynasty, Song Yingxing once described the technical process of mother-coin's sand-copy-casting method in his book *Exploitation of the Works of Nature*: Use four wooden slats of around 0.37 meter long and 4 centimeters wide to make an empty frame as the casting model, fill in fine and smooth soil char powder, scatter a little fir char or willow char on it, or use rosin and boiled oil to fume the model, then lay hundreds of mother-coins on it; again, use the same method to fill another frame, put cover on it and become the back frame of the coin, reverse the two frames, so the mother-coins fall on the back frame; use another filled frame, cover the back frame, reverse; in this way, make out tens of frames and bind them firmly with rope, pour the copper solution into the frame from the hole on the its edge; after cooling, open the frame, then the coins inside appear like branches; clamp the coins one by one and polish them, finally; we get the copper coins.

雕母、母钱、样钱和子钱

雕母：又称"祖钱""雕祖"，是由技艺高超的工匠用铜、锡、牙、木等材料手工雕刻而成的用以铸造母钱的模具。

母钱：由雕母翻铸成的样板钱，是翻砂法铸钱使用的模具。翻铸的母钱被颁发到各地，作为铸钱的范模。

样钱：用母钱翻砂铸成的样板钱，用做铸钱的标准，或进呈供皇帝检验的样品，分为呈样钱、部颁样钱、置样钱、抽样钱。

子钱：由母钱翻铸的流通钱币。

Carved Mother Model, Mother Coin, Sample Coin and Son Coin

Carved Mother Model: It's also called "ancestor coin" and "carved ancestor", which is manually produced by skillful craftsmen with copper, tin, tooth, wood, and other materials to be used for casting mother coin.

Mother Coin: It's the sample coin cast from the carved mother model, and is the model used in sand-copy casting method. The mother coins were issued throughout the nation as the model for casting money.

Sample Coin: It's the sample coin cast from the mother coin, and is used as the casting standard or presented to the emperor for examination, including presented coin, issued coin, setting coin and sampling coin.

Son Coin: The circulated coins cast from the mother coin.

- 咸丰元宝雕母（清）
Carved Mother Model of *Xianfeng* Ingot (Qing Dynasty, 1616-1911)

- 万历通宝白铜样钱（明）
Cupronickel Sample Coin of *Wanli Tongbao* (Ming Dynasty, 1368-1644)

> 古钱币的种类

　　古钱币种类丰富，可以按照各种不同的标准进行划分。

　　按材质不同，古钱币主要分为金属钱币与纸币。金属钱币又可分为金银钱、铜钱、铁钱、铅钱、金银币、铜币、镍币、铝币、铅币等。

　　按形制不同，古钱币可分为贝

隆兴通宝铁钱（南宋）
Longxing Tongbao Iron Money
(Southern Song Dynasty, 1127-1279)

> Types of Chinese Ancient Currencies

Ancient currencies vary in kinds, which can be divided according to different criterions.

　　According to the different materials, it can be divided into metallic currency and paper currency. The former one includes gold and silver money, copper money, iron money, led money, gold and silver coin, copper coin, nickel coin, aluminum coin, lead coin, etc.

　　According to various shapes, it can be divided into shell coin, *Bu* coin, knife-shaped coin, round coin, circular coin (with a square hole), etc.

　　According to different naming methods, it can be divided into weight-named money (cast with coin's weight), value-named money (cast with coin's value or the exchange rate to silver),

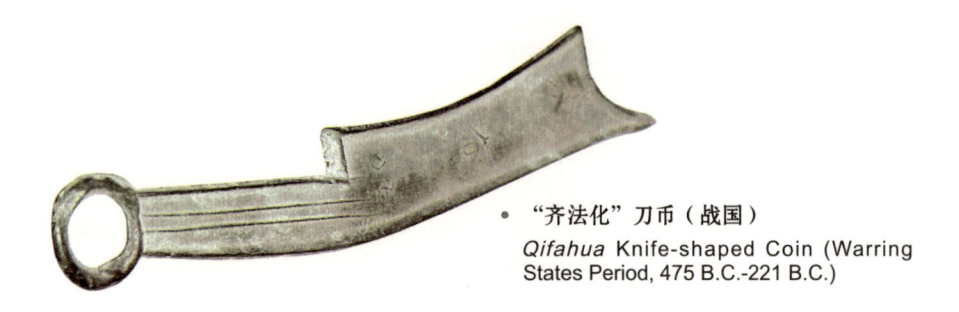

• "齐法化"刀币（战国）
Qifahua Knife-shaped Coin (Warring States Period, 475 B.C.-221 B.C.)

币、布币、刀币、圜钱、方孔圆钱等。

按命名方式不同，古钱币可分为记重钱（铸有重量）、记值钱（铸有价值或对银比价）、年号钱（铸有皇帝年号）、国号钱（铸有国号）、记年钱（铸有铸造年份）、记地钱（铸有铸钱局或地点）等。

按价值划分，古钱币可分为实钱和虚钱。实钱是钱币所代表的价值与本身材料价值相当或接近的钱币；虚钱又称"大钱"，是钱币代表的价值大于本身材料价值的钱币。

按性质划分可分为流通钱币与非流通钱币。流通钱币是在商品交换中承担货币职能的钱币；非流通钱币主要指花钱，在商品交换中不承担货币职能，然而在形制上类似古钱币。

reign title money (cast with the emperor's reign title), dynasty title money (cast with the dynasty title), year money (cast with the foundry year), location money (cast with the casting office or location's name), etc.

According to values, it can be divided into physical money and virtual money. The value of physical money is equal to or similar to its material's value; and virtual money, also called "big money", represents much higher value than its material.

According to properties, it can be divided into circulated money and non-circulated money. Circulated money is the one which possesses the function of money in the exchange; and non-circulated money mainly indicates flower money, which doesn't possesses the money function and is similar to the ancient currency in the shape and form.

花钱

花钱又称"民俗钱币",指具有馈赠、玩赏、佩带、陈列、供奉、随葬等特殊用途,用在非流通领域的纪念性钱币和宗教用钱币等。钱币上多以吉祥话语为装饰,钱文中有星斗、八卦、龙凤、人物等图案。花钱多是民间私铸,材质以铜为主,也有金、银、玉、木、陶、锡、象牙等其他材质,铸造工艺不拘一格,富于装饰性和情趣。常见的花钱如下:

压胜钱——用于避邪的钱币,钱上刻有吉语、符咒等各种图案。

镇库钱——钱局在开炉前,为纪念或避邪而特铸的镇库钱币。

宫钱——宫中节日庆典,用于装饰、庆功赏赐的钱币。

洗儿钱——祝贺生育子女的赠钱。

撒帐钱——婚嫁仪式上分发的赏钱,钱上多铸吉语祝词。

佩钱——佩带在身上的钱币,多铸有各种花纹、吉语、人名、官名等。

供养钱——藏于寺观佛像腹中或悬于佛龛旁,用作供品的钱币。

八卦钱——作为保平安、祛病邪、镇宅院、占卜等用途的钱币,铸有八卦符、咒语、宗教图案等。

冥钱——为死者铸制的殉葬钱币。

打马钱——一种博戏工具,钱上铸有马形、马名,或铸有骑马将军、将军名。

秘戏钱——表现性生活的钱币,铸有男女性交图案。

生肖钱——铸有生肖图案、名称或地支名称的钱币,背文多为八卦、星官、吉语等。

• 压胜钱
Auspicious Money

• 佩钱
Ornament Money

Flower Money

Flower money, also called "folk money", indicates the currencies processing the special functions like gifting, appreciation, wearing, display, worship or as burial objects, as well as the memorial money and religious money used in the non-circulated areas. The currencies regularly are decorated by auspicious words and motifs like stars, the Eight Diagrams, loong, phoenix, figure, etc. Flower money is mainly cast by the folks, mostly with the material of copper, as well as gold, silver, jade, wood, porcelain, tin, ivory, etc. Its casting technique doesn't follow the regular rules and is decorative and full of temperament and interest. The common flower money are as below:

Auspicious Money: It's used for driving away the demon spirits and carved with auspicious words and amulets.

Exorcism Money: Before the casting office starts to operate, in order to commemorate or to avoid evil spirits, people cast the special exorcism money.

Palace Money: It's used to decorate and award in the palace during the festivals and ceremonies.

Washing-Baby Money: It's the gifting money for congratulating the birth of new babies.

Scatter Money: It's the gifting money sent out on the wedding ceremony, with auspicious words carved on it.

Ornament Money: It's the currency decorated on body, mainly with several patterns, auspicious words, names, titles, etc.

Worship Money: it's hidden in the Buddha's belly or hung beside the niche as the offerings.

The Eight Diagrams Money: It's used for keeping safe, avoiding sickness and evil spirits, guarding the yards or divination, with the Eight Diagrams, amulets, religious patterns, etc.

Ming Money: It's used as burial object for the deceased person.

Horse Money: It's a playing tool, and cast with horse shape, horse name, or the general riding a horse and the general's name.

Secret Money: It's used for representing the private daily life, with the pattern of man and woman having sex.

Chinese Zodiac Money: It's cast with the pattern of Chinese zodiac, name or Chinese era, with the Eight Diagrams, deities, and auspicious words cast on the back.

• 八卦钱
The Eight Diagrams Money

• 生肖钱
Chinese Zodiac Money

古钱币鉴赏
Appreciation of Chinese Ancient Currencies

　　中国古钱币发展历史久远，其形制多样、制作原料繁多、工艺多变，而钱币又携带了大量文化信息，所以中国古钱币具有重要的文化艺术价值。如今，古钱币虽已失去了固有的流通价值，然而却留给人们重要的收藏、鉴赏价值。这种鉴赏不仅仅体现在钱币本身形制、制作、文字装饰等方面，还可以通过钱币了解中国古代社会的诸多方面。

Chinese currency boasts a long history and a great variety in designs, materials and techniques. Ancient coins, though no longer serving as currency, are collected and appreciated for their artistic value and the cultural connotations they are carrying. The appreciation of ancient coins, therefore, is not limited to their shapes, manufacturing process and inscription, but extends to the many aspects of ancient societies indicated by each piece of coin.

> 先秦钱币

贝币

贝，原是一种受人喜爱的装饰品，由于其光滑润泽，美观坚固，又便于计量和储存，非常适合充当一般等价物，因此逐渐演化成货币。贝币主要有小孔式、大孔式、背磨式三种，一般穿孔越小者年代越早，原始时期的贝币甚至无孔。背磨式贝币是将背部磨去，只保留腹部，属于年代稍晚的品种。贝币还经常被用作赏赐品和随葬品，在商周的铜器上就有许多关于赏贝的记载，同时期的贵族墓葬中也多有贝币出土。

随着青铜冶铸业的发展，贝币中出现了最重要的品种——铜贝。铜贝是中国最早的金属铸币，一直

> Currencies of the Pre-Qin Period (approx. 2070 B.C.-221 B.C.)

Shell Coins

Originally regarded as ideal decorations for their smooth and sleek appearance, shells were later used as money because they were hard and easy to count and store, satisfying as a universal equivalent. There are shells with a small hole, those with a big hole and those with their back abraded. A smaller hole suggests an earlier age of production, while shells used in the primitive times have no holes at all. Back-abraded shells, with their back abraded and belly left, are products of a relatively late time. Shells were also often used as rewards or funeral objects. A lot of records about the appreciation of shells are inscribed on bronze ware of the Shang Dynasty (1600B.C.-1046B.C.),

贝币（西周）
Shell Coins (Western Zhou Dynasty, 1046B.C.-771 B.C.)

流通到秦始皇废贝行钱。铜贝一般为青铜质，外形似天然海贝，有无文铜贝和蚁鼻钱（有铭铜贝）两种。

无文铜贝面鼓凸，一般都铸有一道弯形齿槽，背部中空，不铸铭文，铸行于商代晚期至战国早期，在黄河中下游地区流通。战国早期前后，出现了包金、包银的无文铜贝，铸作精致，多为王侯贵族使用，计量单位为"锊"，一锊近十二铢（约8克）。1976年，在河南安阳殷墟出土的无文铜贝，距今已有三千多年的历史，是世界上最早的金属货币。

有铭铜贝面微凸起，呈椭圆形，顶端铸有穿孔，有些穿孔不透，

and shell coins have been unearthed from tombs of Shang's nobilities.

The development of bronze metallurgy brought about the most important variety of shell coin, the bronze shell coin, the earliest Chinese metallic money which was in use until Emperor Shihuang (259 B.C.-210 B.C.) of the Qin Dynasty (221 B.C.-206 B.C.) abolished the use of shell coins and initiated that of *Ban-Liang* coins. Bronze shell coins are imitations of seashell, and including two kinds: insciptionless bronze shell coin and *Yibi* coin (inscription bronze shell coin).

Bronze shell coins without inscriptions have a bulging hollow back and a curved aperture toothed at the edges. They were cast between the late Shang Dynasty and the early Warring

- 包金铜贝（春秋）

包金铜贝是在铜贝上包裹一层黄金薄片。出土的包金铜贝在绿锈斑驳中露出金色，甚为美观。

Gilded Bronze Shell Coins (Spring and Autumn Period, 770 B.C.-476 B.C.)

Those unearthed bronze shell coins, covered with a gold foil, appeal greatly to the eye with gold shining through the patinated surface.

只存孔形。背面铸有阴文铭文，铭文有"忻""紊""金""咒""君""巽"等，与穿孔组合在一起，像一只蚂蚁歇在鼻尖上，故俗称"蚁鼻钱"。蚁鼻钱铸行于春秋晚期至战国末年的楚国，流通于江淮流域。在铸行后期，蚁鼻钱的钱文统一为"咒"字，因"咒"字极像鬼脸，又称"鬼脸钱"。

States Period (475 B.C.-221 B.C.) and circulated in areas along the middle and lower streams of the Yellow River. Exquisitely manufactured inscriptionless bronze shell coins rolled with gold or silver appeared in about the early Warring States Period and were used by royal families and the nobilities. The unit of such bronze shells was *Lüe* (锊), which equaled twelve *Zhu* (铢, about eight grams). The inscriptionless bronze shell coins unearthed on the site of Yin Ruins, ruins of the Shang Dynasty, in Anyang, Henan in 1976 were the earliest metallic money in the world, which date back to 3,000 years ago.

Inscribed bronze shell coins are egg-shaped, with a moderately bulging belly and a hole, thorough or half-done, at the narrower end. They are inscribed with characters like 忻 (*Xin*, joy or enlightenment), 紊 (*Wen*, disorder), 金 (*Jin*, gold), 咒 (*Zhou*, curse), 君 (*Jun*, the King) and 巽 (*Xun*, wind, assistance or modesty), combining with the hole, which seems like an ant resting on the tip of a nose, hence the name ant-nose coin, *Yibi* coin. Those bronze shell coins were cast between the late Spring and Autumn Period and the late Warring States Period in the state Chu, circulating in areas along the Yangtze River and Huai River. Inscriptions on those items were later standardized to the character "咒" (amulet), which looks like a ghost's face, and therefore the ant nose coin is also called the "ghost-face coin".

- 鬼脸钱（战国）
Ghost-face Coin (Warring States Period, 475 B.C.-221 B.C.)

蚁鼻钱

蚁鼻，本喻轻小。晋代葛洪《抱朴子·论仙》载："以蚁鼻之缺，捐无价之淳钧。"意思是说只因轻微的缺陷，就舍弃了无价的淳钧宝剑。可见蚁鼻钱也可指小钱，这种有铭铜贝可能是属于比较零碎的小钱。

Yibi Coin

The name *Yibi* could also mean ant's nose, which indicates the quality of being light and small. Ge Hong of the Jin Dynasty (265-420) explains in *On Immortality* in *Baopuzi* (*The Master Who Embraces Simplicity*) that "The priceless sword Chunjun (a famous ancient sword) was discarded for an ant-nose aw." *Yibi* coin, the inscribed bronze shell coin, was probably used as loose change.

- 蚁鼻钱（战国）
Yibi Coin(Warring States Period, 475 B.C.-221 B.C.)

布币

铜贝流通的同时,在农业比较发达的黄河中游地区,因生产的需要,出现了一种青铜铲形农具,称作"钱"和"镈"。由于青铜本身的价值,这种农具一问世,就兼具一般等价物的职能。随着青铜业和手工业的发展,"钱"和"镈"发生了重大的变化——"钱"逐渐成为通行货币的总称,不再是特指的农具;"镈"的体型缩小,因"布"与"镈"古音相通,布币由此诞生。

布币又称"布钱""布",始铸于春秋而盛行于战国,到秦始皇统一货币止,行用了五百年左右。

Bu Coins, or the Spade Coins

When bronze shell coins were in use, bronze *Bu* coin named *Qian* and *Bo* were invented in agriculturally developed areas along the mid-stream of the Yellow River. Because of the intrinsic value of bronze, these farm tools were born with the identity of universal equivalents. The development of bronze metallurgy and handicraft industry led to significant changes to *Qian* and *Bo*, the former becoming the collective name for money instead of a particular agricultural implement, while the latter shrinking into a portable object which came to be known as *Bu* coin, which was then pronounced the same as *Bo*.

Bu coin, also called as "*Bu* money" or "*Bu*", was originally cast in the Spring and Autumn Period and prevalent during the Warring States Period. They were in use for about 500 years until Emperor Qin Shihuang standardized currency. *Bu* coins mainly circulated in the capital city

• 斜肩弧足空首布(春秋)
布币上铸有"卢氏"二字,为地名。
Hollow-headed *Bu* Coin with Sloping Shoulders and Arched Crutch (Spring and Autumn Period, 770 B.C.-476 B.C.)
The two characters inscribed on the coin, 卢氏 (*Lushi*), are a name of a place which is present Lushi County in Henan Province.

布币流通的地区主要是周朝的京畿之地、春秋的秦和三晋地区，以及战国的韩、赵、魏、燕等国，相当于现在的山西、陕西、河南、河北、山东、辽宁等地。布币多为私铸币，轻重、大小不一，文字书写随意，不追求艺术性。币上铸有币值、重量、地名等内容，以记载地名的居多，是中国钱币史上最早铸有文字的金属货币。

布币种类繁多，根据布首、布肩、布裆和布足的变化，主要分为原始布、空首布、平首布三种。

of Zhou Dynasty (1046 B.C.-256 B.C.) and its environs, the state Qin and the Sanjin area in the Spring and Autumn Period, and the warring states like Han, Zhao, Wei and Yan, which are roughly the present Shanxi, Shaanxi, Henan, Hebei, Shandong and Liaoning. The casting of *Bu* coin wasn't supervised by the government and have no limit on the standard of weight, size and inscription, or to the artistic value. Inscription on these coins indicates value, weight or, in most cases, a place. *Bu* coins were the earliest Chinese metallic coins with inscription.

布币各部位的名称

首：布的上端，有空首和平首之分。

銎：空首布首部的空隙部位。

身：布首以外的实体部分。

肩：布首之下两侧的横向部位，有平肩、圆肩、耸肩、斜肩等。

腰：布身中部两侧的部位，有直腰、束腰之分。

裆：两足相接的内凹部位，有平裆、直裆、弧裆、三角形裆等。

足：布身下端的两个角，有弧足、方足、尖足、圆足等。

• 平肩弧足空首布
Hollow-headed *Bu* Coin with Square Shoulders and Arched Crutch

Parts' Names of *Bu* Coin

Head: It is either hollow or flat, which is the upper part of a *Bu* coin.

Socket: It is the hole in the hollowed head.

Body: It is the solid part of the *Bu* coin except the head.

Shoulders: They are the parts below the head which run athwart. The shoulders can be square, arched, pointed or sloping.

Waist: It is the middle part of a *Bu* coin, which is either straight or narrowed.

Crutch: It is the part between the legs where they join the body, which can be square, straight, arched or gabled.

Feet: They are the two protruding lower parts, which can be arched, square, pointed or round.

原始布

又称"大铲布",铸行于商代中晚期至西周中晚期,是最早的布币。其形制粗糙,还未脱离农具的形状,没有统一的形制标准,銎短体大,多不铸铭文,少数铸有直纹、斜纹和"益""卢氏"(地名,今河南省卢氏县)等文字。

空首布

空首布,在《辞海》中的解释是有銎的布币。"銎"是指铲子上安柄的孔,所以空首布的特征就是在布首有一个可安柄的中空的銎。空首布作为一种早期的布币已经完全脱离了农具的造型。其由春秋时

The various *Bu* coins are classified, according to the variations of the head, shoulders, crutch and feet, into the prototype *Bu* coin, the hollow-headed *Bu* coin and the flat-headed *Bu* coin.

Prototype *Bu* Coins

This type of *Bu* coin is also known as the big *Bu*, which was cast between the mid Shang Dynasty and late Western Zhou Dynasty and was the earliest *Bu* money. It is crude, large, short-headed, and similar in shape to the original agricultural implement. There was no standard for its shape and size. Most of the prototype *Bu* coins are not inscribed, and a few bear an inscription of vertical lines, diagonal lines or characters like 益 (*Yi*) and 卢氏 (*Lushi*).

- **平肩弧足空首布（春秋）**

  平肩弧足空首布两肩平直，足内凹呈弧形，长銎，銎内留有范芯。其面背多铸三道平行竖纹，或中间一道竖纹、两侧各一道斜纹。有大、小两种形制，铭文有180余种，包括地名、数目、干支、阴阳五行、方位、吉语、事物等。

  Hollow-headed *Bu* Coin with Square Shoulders and Arched Crutch (Spring and Autumn Period, 770 B.C.-476 B.C.)

  This type of coin has square shoulders, an arched crutch and a deep socket with part of the mould in the head. Usually three parallel lines or the pattern of a vertical line between two diagonal lines is inscribed on the obverse and reverse. There are two standards for the size, the big and the small, and over 180 kinds of inscription, including place names, numbers, times, *Yin, Yang* and the Five Elements (metal, wood, water, fire and earth), directions, auspicious phrases and objects.

- **斜肩弧足空首布（春秋）**

  斜肩弧足空首布两肩向外倾斜，足下端呈圆弧状，銎较短。其面铸两道斜纹，背铸两道斜纹，斜纹间有一道竖纹。有大、小两种形制，铭文有"武""卢氏""三川釿"等。

  Hollow-headed *Bu* Coin with Sloping Shoulders and Arched Crutch (Spring and Autumn Period, 770 B.C.-476 B.C.)

  This type of coin has sloping shoulders, an arched crutch and a short socket in the head. The pattern of a vertical line between two diagonal lines is inscribed on the obverse and reverse, as well as some place names like 武 (*Wu*), 卢氏 (*Lushi*) and 三川釿 (*Sanchuanjin*). There are also two size standards of it.

- **耸肩尖足空首布（春秋 晋）**

  耸肩尖足空首布多素面，无文字，故又称"无文大布"。其两肩耸起，与币身中线构成斜角，足下端尖锐，长銎，銎有穿孔，背有三道竖纹，薄而大，有大、小两种形制。少数铸有简单文字，多为数字、干支、地名等。

  Hollow-headed *Bu* Coin with Pointed Shoulders and Pointed Feet, State Jin (Spring and Autumn Period, 770 B.C.-476 B.C.)

  This type of coin is usually not inscribed with characters, so it is also called as "inscriptionless big *Bu* coin". They are cast with pointed shoulders which run oblique to the axis of the coin, pointed feet and a long head with a socket. There are three vertical lines inscribed on the reverse. It's thin and big, having two forms of big and small. And occasionally simple characters are inscribed indicating number, time and place.

期的周、晋、郑、卫等国铸行，从殷商至战国流通了一千多年。

　　空首布一般均铸有铭文，布面铸一字、二字或多字铭文，内容有记数、记干支、记天象、记地名等。空首布形制大小不一，早期空首布体大、精整，后期则变得又轻又小。

　　根据造型的不同，空首布又可分为平肩弧足空首布、斜肩弧足空首布、耸肩尖足空首布三类。

平首布

　　随着工艺的改进，在空首布的基础上简化而来的平首布逐渐成为主流。相对于空首布而言，平首布

Hollow-headed *Bu* Coins

According to *Cihai*, the *Great Chinese Dictionary*, the hollow-headed *Bu* coin is a *Bu* coin which has a socket in its head by which a wood pole could be attached. This socket is the unique feature of this type of *Bu* coin, which, used as money, no longer retained the size or shape of a farm tool. Hollow-headed *Bu* coins were cast in States of Zhou, Jin, Zheng and Wei in the Spring and Autumn Period, and were in use for more than 1,000 years from the Shang Dynasty to the Warring States Period.

　　Hollow-headed *Bu* coins were mostly inscribed with one, two or several characters, telling about value, time,

- **平首尖足布（战国 赵）**
  平首尖足布由耸肩尖足空首布演变而来，平首，耸肩或平肩，平裆或弧裆，尖足。布首有两道竖纹。有大、小两种形制，铭文丰富，有60多种，多为地名。
  Flat-headed *Bu* Coin with Pointed Feet, State Zhao (Warring States Period, 475 B.C.-221 B.C.)
  This type of coin has evolved from the *Bu* coin with pointed shoulders, pointed feet and a hollow head, and has a flat head, pointed or square shoulders, a square or arched crutch and pointed feet. There are two vertical lines on the head, two size standards for casting, and 60 kinds of inscription, most of which being place names.

• 平首方足布（战国 韩）

平首方足布平首，平肩或圆肩，方足，平档或圆档。布面有一道直纹，上通于首，铭文在直纹左右，多为地名。形制庞杂，可分为平肩平档方足布、圆肩圆档方足布、平首圆档方足布。

Flat-headed *Bu* Coin with Square Feet, State Han (Warring States Period, 475 B.C.-221 B.C.)

This type of coin has a flat head, square or round shoulders, square feet and a square or arched crutch. On the obverse is inscribed a straight line which runs through the head and on either side of which are inscribed characters, mostly place names. There are three sub-divisions of the flat-headed square foot coin, that with square shoulders and a square crutch, that with round shoulders and an arched crutch and that with square shoulders and an arched crutch.

的首部已没有可以安柄的銎，形体也较小，重量也较轻。平首布主要铸造于战国时期，流通于三晋和燕国地区。

按照形制的不同，平首布可以分为平首尖足布、平首方足布、圆首圆足布和异形平首布四类。其中异形平首布为平首、平肩、方足，布首部两侧各有一个锐角，故也称"锐角方足布"。有大、小两种形制，铭文有"垂""公""金涅""卢氏金涅""俞金涅"等。1981年，河南鹤壁出土了三千余枚异形平首布，具有重要的历史价值。

celestial phenomenon or place. The size of a coin varies from the neat bigness in its early employment to the lightness and small size in a later time.

Hollow-headed *Bu* coins are divided into three groups, that with square shoulders and an arched crutch, that with sloping shoulders and an arched crutch and that with pointed shoulders and pointed feet.

Flat-headed *Bu* Coins

Thanks to the advanced handicraft, the flat-headed *Bu* coins simplified from their hollow-headed precedent gradually prevailed. They have lost the hollow head of the early *Bu*, and are smaller and lighter. Flat-headed *Bu* coins were

- 圆首圆足布（战国 赵）

圆首圆足布圆首、圆肩、圆裆、圆足。布面铭文多为地名，背平素或铸有"五""廿六"等数字。其中有一种布首和两足各铸一圆形穿孔的三孔布，以"铢""两"为计量单位，铸造精良，面文多为地名，背文多记重和记值，如"一两"或"十二铢"等，存世稀少，目前仅出土两枚半（一枚残损），为先秦货币中的珍品。

Bu Coin with Round Head and Round Feet, State Zhao (Warring States Period, 475 B.C.-221 B.C.)

The head, shoulders, crutch and feet of this type of coin are all round. The obverse is usually inscribed with place names, while the reverse is either left blank or inscribed with numerals like 五 (five) and 廿六 (twenty six). In the round shouldered round foot *Bu* coin family there is a three-holed *Bu* coin, which has a hole in the head and each foot. The unit of this coin is *Zhu* (铢) or *Liang* (两). The three-holed *Bu* coin is exquisitely cast and inscribed on the obverse with a place name and on the reverse with the weight and value of the coin, such as one *Liang* and twelve *Zhu*. It is a rare type among the coins of the pre-Qin Dynasty, and so far only two and a half (a mutilated one) have been found.

mainly cast during the Warring States Period and circulated in Sanjin area and the State Yan.

Flat-headed *Bu* coins are distinguished into four classes, that with pointed feet, that with square feet, that with a round head and round feet and that of an irregular shape with a at head, square shoulders and feet and a small triangular projection on either side of the head, which gives this coin the name "sharp-cornered *Bu*". There are two size standards for this type of coin, and the inscription usually includes a place name and the characters 金 (*Jin*) and 涅 (*Nie*), the former meaning metal while the later probably money, like 垂 (*Chui*), 公 (*Gong*), 金涅 (*Jinnie*), 卢氏金涅 (*Lushi Jinnie*) and 俞金涅 (*Yu Jinnie*). In 1981, more than 3000 irregular flat-headed *Bu* coins were unearthed in Hebi, Henan Province, which bore great archaeological value.

Knife-shaped Coins

Knife-shaped coins are the general name of the knife-shaped coins cast and used during the Spring and Autumn Period and the Warring States Period. Their ancestor was a kind of knife used by the nomads

刀币

刀币是春秋战国时期铸行的各种刀形货币的总称,起源于中国古代山戎、北狄等北方游牧民族渔猎用的一种捕鱼刀具。有的刀币上还画有鱼纹,成为刀币起源的实物例证。还有一种说法是刀币源于古代的一种文具"削刀",用来刮制简册或删改竹简上的错字。春秋前期,齐国最早开始模仿生产工具铜刀,铸行了自己的金属货币。燕、赵两国在其影响下也开始铸造,于是在现在的华北地区流通起刀币。

in the North, such as the Shanrong and Beidi peoples, to catch fish, which can be attested to by the fish patterns on some knife-shaped coins. Another explanation has it that the knife-shaped coin originated as an ancient stationery tool used to polish bamboo slips for writing or to scrape away an error. The State Qi in the early Spring and Autumn Period was the first to mould metallic coins after bronze knives and initiate its own money, which was followed suit by the States of Yan and Zhao. As a result, knife-shaped coins began to circulate in areas which are in present North China.

- 青铜削刀(春秋)
Bronze Cutting Knife (Spring and Autumn Period, 475 B.C.-221 B.C.)

刀币各部位的名称

首:刀尖部位,有尖首、圆首或平首之分。
刃:刃口呈曲凹状,无锋。
面:正面部位。
背:与刀刃相对应的部位,呈反张形,有直背、弧背、磬折(曲折如磬形)之分。
身:中间部位,是刀币的主体部分,多轻薄。
柄:把手部位,多铸有两道平行的直纹。
环:刀柄下端的圆环,多扁薄。

Names of Each Part of Knife-shaped Coin

Tip: It is the end of the blade, which can be pointed, round or square.

Edge: It is the edge of the blade, which is inwardly curved and not sharpened.

Face: It is the obverse of the coin.

Back: It is the back of the blade, which can be straight, curved or in ected.

Body: It is the main part of the coin, which is usually light and thin.

Haft: It is usually inscribed with two parallel straight lines.

Ring: It is at and thin, at the end of the haft.

- 安阳之大刀（战国 齐）
  Big Knife-shaped Coin of Anyang, State Qi (Warring States Period, 475 B.C.-221 B.C.)

因为铸行时代和流通范围的不同，刀币在形制、重量及铭文上存有差异。根据刀首形制的不同，可将刀币分为齐刀、尖首刀、针首刀、明刀和直刀等。

齐刀

齐刀，铸行于齐国，因刀面有"化"字，又称"刀化"。齐刀以厚重精美著称，尖首、弧背、凹刃，有边郭，刀环周正饱满，形体

The shape, weight and inscription of the knife-shaped coin vary with different times of casting and areas of circulation. Knife-shaped coins are divided according to their shapes into the Qi knife-shaped coin, pointed tip knife-shaped coin, needle tip knife-shaped coin, *Ming* knife-shaped coin and straight knife-shaped coin.

Qi Knife-shaped Coins

Qi knife-shaped coins were cast and circulated in the State Qi. Because of

较大，有"齐大刀"之称。刀面文字多为地名加"法化"二字。"法化"指重量、成色、大小均符合标准的标准货币。刀背上端饰有三道平行的横线纹，下端有星纹、文字和标记等。依照刀面铭文的多少，分为三字刀、四字刀、五字刀和六字刀等。

目前发现的齐刀有齐大刀（三字刀）、齐之大刀（四字刀）、安阳之大刀（安阳五字刀）、即墨大刀（即墨四字刀）、节墨之大刀（节墨五字刀）、齐返邦长大刀（六字刀）六种。

- 齐返邦长大刀（战国 齐）
Qi Fanbang Changdadao, State Qi (Warring States Period, 475 B.C.-221 B.C.)

the character 化 (*Hua*) inscribed on the obverse, those knife-shaped coins are also called the *Hua* knives, meaning knife money. Qi knife-shaped coins are known for their thickness, weightiness and exquisite handicraft. Those knives, named the big knife-shaped coin of Qi for their largeness, have a pointed tip, arched back, concave blade edge, a perfect ring and a raised rim. The obverse is usually inscribed with the characters 法化 (*Fahua*, 法 means legal), which informs that those knife-shaped coins were cast in conformity with the standard weight, alloy and size. On the reverse, three parallel horizontal lines are inscribed on the upper part, with stars, characters and symbols inscribed below. They are known as three character knives, four character knives and so on, according to the number of characters in their inscriptions.

Up to now people have found six kinds of Qi knives, inscribed respectively with characters 齐大刀 (*Qi Dadao*, the big knife of Qi), 齐之大刀 (*Qi Zhi Dadao*, the big knife of Qi), 安阳之大刀 (*Anyang Zhi Dadao*, the big knife of Anyang), 即墨大刀 (*Jimo Dadao*, the big knife of Jimo, a place in Qi), 节墨之大刀 (*Jiemo Zhi Dadao*, the big knife

尖首刀

尖首刀，铸行于燕国，是燕国早期流通的钱币。刀首尖锐，故名。刀首或长或短，弧背，凹刃，刀身隆起，有边郭，中断于与柄相交处，刀柄细，略有弧度，柄面背多有一条或两条纵线，刀环为圆形或椭圆形。钱文多为一个字，有"王""囚""上""父"等字。

针首刀

针首刀是北部山戎仿尖首刀而铸造的一种刀币，因刀首尖锐如针而得名。针首刀的外郭弧度大，刀身单薄，有郭隆起，刀柄纤细，柄面有两道纵纹，柄背有一道纵纹，刀环扁小，多竖椭圆形或圆形。钱文或面或背，不固定，多

of Jiemo, another name for Jimo) and 齐返邦长大刀 (*Qi Fanbang Chang Dadao*, the long, big knife cast in celebration of the King's return to the capital). They are also named according to the number of characters inscribed.

Pointed Tip Knife-shaped Coins

Those knife-shaped coins were cast in the State Yan and circulated in the early period of Yan. They are distinguished by a pointed tip, which has no standard length. The back is arched and the edge of the blade concave. The body is heaved, with a rim which ends at the joint with the narrow and slightly curved haft. Usually there is one or two vertical lines inscribed on the haft. The ring is either round or ellipse. Usually a single character is inscribed, such as 王 (*Wang*,

- 尖首刀（战国）
Pointed Tip Knife-shaped Coin (Warring States Period, 475 B.C.-221 B.C.)

- 针首刀（战国）
Needle Tip Knife-shaped Coin (Warring States Period, 475 B.C.-221 B.C.)

为象形文字。

明刀

明刀，铸行于战国时期的燕国。其正面铸有一个符号，形似甲骨文中的"日""月"二字，日月二字合起来即"明"字，故称"明刀"。也有学者认为该符号为古"匽"，匽为燕国都城，这一说法更具说服力。

明刀由小型尖首刀演变而来，经历了形制由大到小，刀背从弧背到折背，面文由斜目形到平目形的发展过程。明刀流通地域很广，在河北、辽宁、吉林、河南等地都曾出土，朝鲜、日本等国也有发现。

• 明刀（战国 燕）
Ming Knife-shaped Coin, State Yan (Warring States Period, 475 B.C.-221 B.C.)

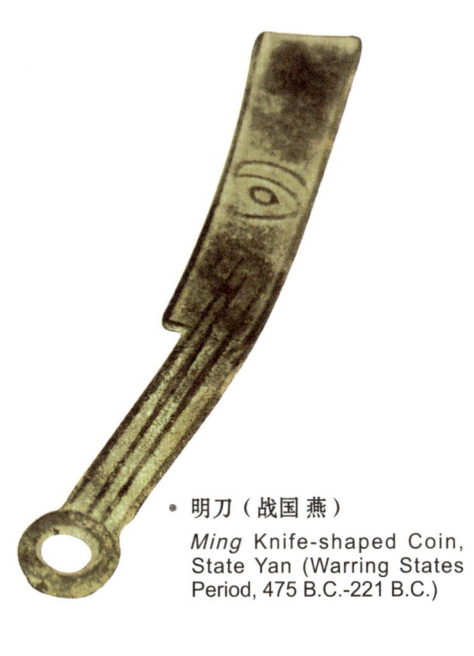

the King), 囚 (*Qiu*, the prisoner), 上 (*Shang*, the above or the superior, which may refer to heaven or to the King) and 父 (*Fu*, the father).

Needle Tip Knife-shaped Coins

Those knife-shaped coins were cast in imitation of the needle tip knives used by the Shanrong people in the north. The tip is longer and more pointed than that of a pointed tip knife-shaped coin. The back is much curved, the blade is thin and with a raised outline, and the haft is narrow. There are two vertical lines on the obverse of the haft, and one on the reverse. The ring is small and flat, usually ellipse or round. Characters, inscribed either on the obverse or the reverse of the coin, are mostly hieroglyphs.

Ming Knife-shaped Coins

Ming knife-shaped coins were cast and circulated in the State Yan in the Warring States Period. The symbol inscribed on the obverse resembles the two hieroglyphic characters 日 (*Ri*, the sun) and 月 (*Yue*, the moon), which combined form the character 明 (*Ming*, brightness), hence the name *Ming* knife-shaped coins. But it is more persuasive that, according to some scholars, the symbol resembles the character 匽 (*Yan*) in its ancient form,

根据形制的不同，明刀主要分为弧背刀和方折刀两种。

弧背刀又称"圆折刀"，体形较大，刀身圆折，刀身与刀柄连接处呈弧形，弧背凹刃，刀首宽于刀身，刀柄上的直纹到刀身即止。刀面钱文有一个"燕"字，背文较多样，有"左""右""内""外""中"等字。

方折刀又称"磬折刀"，体形较小，刀身与刀柄连接处方折，直背直刃，刀身方折，像古磬形状。钱文字体雄伟长大，有"工""左匽下""右邑""匽八""匽邑外炉"等字。

直刀

直刀又称"赵刀""圆首刀"，铸行于赵国和中山国。其形体轻薄，刀首圆钝，刀身直，刀刃和刀背略有弧度，刀柄有一至两道纵纹，或无纹，刀环呈椭圆形或圆形。

直刀有大、中、小三种形制。其面文多铸地名，如"甘丹"（赵国都城，河北邯郸西南）、"白人"（柏人，赵国重镇，今河北隆尧县境内）、"蔺"（赵国地名，今山西柳林县北，一说在陕西渭南

which was the name of the capital of the State Yan (written as 燕).

Evolving from a small pointed tip knife, the *Ming* knife has gone through changes from a big size to a small one, curved back to inflected one and the inscription of an oblique eye to that of a horizontal one. *Ming* knife-shaped coins circulated widely and many have been unearthed in Hebei, Liaoning, Jilin and Henan, and even as far afield as North Korea and Japan.

Ming knives are divided into two groups, that with a curved back and that with an inflected back. The former is larger, arched at the back as well as the joint of the blade and haft, and concave at the edge of the blade. It has a blade wider at the head than at the part near the haft. The straight line inscription on the haft ends as it reaches the blade. On the obverse of the blade there is a inscribed character 燕 (*Yan*, the State Yan), while on the reverse the character may be 左 (*Zuo*, left), 右 (*You*, right), 内 (*Nei*, inside), 外 (*Wai*, outside) or 中 (*Zhong*, centre). The inflected back knife-shaped coin, on the other hand, is smaller and bent at the part where the blade joins the haft to form a protruding angle, and the back of the blade is straight. This shape is known as *Qing* (磬), a chime stone. They are inscribed characters like 工 (*Gong*), 左匽下 (*Zuoyanxia*), 右邑 (*Youyi*), 匽八 (*Yanba*) or 匽邑外炉 (*Yanyiwailu*), and are big and of a vigorous beauty.

Straight Knife-shaped Coins

Issued in the states of Zhao and Zhongshan (encompassed by Zhao), the straight knives are also known as the Zhao knives or the round head knives. They are light, thin, and straight, with a round tip and a blade only slightly curved. There is one or two vertical lines on the haft, or no lines inscribed at all. The ring is ellipse or round.

There are three size standards for the straight knife-shaped coins, the big, the middle and the small. Inscription on the obverse is usually a place name, such as 甘丹 (*Gandan*, capital city of Zhao, which is present southwest Handan in Hebei), 白人 (*Bairen*, important strategic spot of Zhao, which is in present Longyao in Hebei), 蔺 (*Lin*, a place of Zhao, which is present north of Liulin in Shanxi, or, according to another explanation, northwest Weinan in Shaanxi) and 晋阳 (*Jinyang*, one-time capital of Zhao, which is present Jinyuan in southwest Taiyuan in Shanxi). The reverse is often left blank or occasionally

- "成白"直刀石钱范
  Stone Model of *Chengbai* Straight Knife-shaped Coin

- 直刀（战国 中山国）
  1979年，河北灵寿中山国故都城址内，出土的铭文为"成白"的直刀与石钱范。
  Straight Knife-shaped Coin, State Zhongshan (Warring States Period, 475 B.C.-221 B.C.)
  Both were unearthed in 1979 on the site of the capital of the State Zhongshan, in Lingshou, Hebei Province.

西北）、"晋阳"（曾为赵国都城，今山西太原西南晋源镇）等，背多平素，少数有一字，为记数目或记天干。直刀多出土于河北、山西、内蒙古等地。

inscribed with one character indicating a number or time. Straight knives are mostly found in Heibei, Shanxi and Inner Mongolia.

常见的钱文书体
Common Calligraphic Styles of Coin Inscriptions

古钱币的钱文书体风格多样，展现出中国书法艺术的独特魅力，不少钱文还出自名家之手，极为珍贵。

There is a good diversity in the handwriting style of the inscription on ancient coins, demonstrating unique charm of Chinese calligraphy. Many an inscription was molded after the handwriting of great calligraphists, which was of inestimable value.

甲骨文、钟鼎文

先秦钱币的钱文书体是甲骨文和钟鼎文，此时文字尚未统一，诸侯列国均铸有钱币，蚁鼻钱、布币、刀币、圜钱上的文字有繁有简，风采各异。

Oracle Bone Script (*Jiaguwen*) and Bronze Inscription (*Zhongdingwen*)

Calligraphic styles in pre-Qin times were exemplified by the oracle bone script and the inscriptions on bronze bells and cauldrons. There was no standardized writing system, and money issued by different states, namely the ant-nose shells, *Bu* coins, knife-shaped coins and round coins, were then inscribed with characters of a variety of styles.

• 钟鼎文"蔺"圆首圆足布（战国 赵）
Bu Coin with Round Head and Round Feet, Inscribed with the Character 蔺 in the Bronze Inscription Style, State Zhao (Warring States Period, 475 B.C.-221 B.C.)

小篆

秦统一中国后，丞相李斯简化大篆书体为小篆。秦"半两"钱的钱文是小篆"半两"二字，由李斯书。小篆作为钱文书体一直沿用至魏晋南北朝。

Small Seal Script (*Xiaozhuan*)

After Qin unified China, prime minister Li Si simplified the large or great seal script (*Dazhuan*) into the small seal script. The characters 半两 (*Ban-Liang*, half *Liang*) on the Qin coin was written by Li Si in the small seal script, which had been used for coin inscription until the Southern and Northern dynasties (220-589).

• 小篆"半两"钱（秦）
Ban-Liang Coin, Inscribed in Small Seal Script (Qin Dynasty, 221 B.C.-206 B.C.)

隶书

隶书体的钱文出现在东晋十六国时期。如十六国时期成汉皇帝李寿铸的"汉兴"钱，面文"汉兴"两字用隶书书写。唐代钱文中的隶书始于"开元通宝"钱，钱文由书法家欧阳询书写。五代十国至北宋的钱文书体，也多为隶书。

Clerical Style (*Lishu*)

Coins with clerical style inscription appeared in the Eastern Jin Dynasty (317-420). Emperor of the Cheng-Han State, Li Shou, for example, authorized the casting of coins inscribed with the characters 汉兴 (*Hangxing*, meaning prosperity for Han) in the clerical style. Coin inscription in clerical style in the Tang Dynasty (618-907) stemmed from the round coin inscribed with 开元通宝 (*Kaiyuan Tongbao*, the inaugural currency of the Tang Dynasty, first cast in 621) which were written by the calligraphy master Ouyang Xun. Coin inscriptions from the Five dynasties and Ten states (907-979) to the Northern Song Dynasty (960-1127) were mostly written in the clerical style.

• 隶书"开元通宝"鎏金钱（唐）
Gilded Round Coin Inscribed with "开元通宝" in the Clerical Style (Tang Dynasty, 618-907)

宋体

从南宋淳熙七年（1180年）的"淳熙元宝"起，钱文逐渐统一为宋体字。

Song Style

Coin inscription had been gradually standardized to the Song style since the issue of the *Chunxi Yuanbao* in the 7th year of the Chunxi Period (1180) in the Southern Song Dynasty.

- 宋体"淳熙元宝"（南宋）
Chunxi Yuanbao in Song Style (Southern Song Dynasty, 1127-1279)

圜钱

圜钱又称"圜金"或"环钱"，圆形，中央有一圆孔或方孔，铸行于战国中晚期，是战国时期最为先进的金属铸币。战国中期以后，各国纷纷铸行圜钱，币呈现圆形化趋势。有人认为圜钱是由璧、环演化而来的，也有人认为是从古时纺车的纺轮发展而来。而从货币形制的发展来看，钱币向圆形

Round Coins

Round coins are coins with a round outline and a round or square hole in the middle. They were first cast during the mid and late Warring States Period and were the most advanced metallic money at that time. The mid Warring States Period marked the beginning of a tendency of the coin outline toward roundness as the states began to cast round coins. It is believed by some that

- 玉璧（良渚文化）
圆形圆孔的璧和纺轮都有可能是圜钱的起源器形。
Jade *Bi* (*Liangzhu* Culture, 3300 B.C.-2200 B.C.)
Both *Bi* and the spinning wheel, with their round outline and round hole, could have been the ancestor of the round coin.

• 陶纺轮（新石器时代）
Earthen Spinning Wheels (Neolithic Age, approx. 8500-4500 Years Ago)

发展是必然的结果，因为圆形钱币铸造工艺简单，成品率高，且适合反复地流通。

圜钱形体小，通常钱面铸有铭文，背光素。圜钱有三种计量单位，分别是以"两"为单位的秦国圜钱，以"釿"为单位的两周、三晋地区的圜钱，以"化"为单位的齐、燕圜钱。

依据穿孔形制的不同，圜钱可分为圆形圆孔圜钱和圆形方孔圜钱。

圆形圆孔圜钱

穿孔为圆形的圜钱，是圜钱中较早的形态，铸行于战国中晚期的魏、赵及秦国。圆孔大小因时间早晚有所不同，早期圆孔较小，晚期圆孔较大。

round coins have evolved from *Bi* (璧, an ancient circular jade artifact) and *Huan* (环, jade ring or bracelet), and by others from the ancient spinning wheel. The tendency toward a round outline was inevitable for the development of coinage, for round coins were not only easier to cast and therefore guaranteed a high pass rate in production, but suitable for repeated circulation.

Round coins are small, usually inscribed on the obverse and blank on the reverse. There were three units of round coins, the *Liang* (两) of the Qin coin, *Jin* (釿) of the coins circulating in the capital area of the Western and Eastern Zhou dynasties as well as Sanjin area, and *Hua* (化) referred to the coins used in the States of Qi and Yan.

Round coins are divided into two groups, that with a round hole and that with a square one.

Round-holed Round Coins

Round-holed round coins were a precursor of the round coin family, cast in the states of Wei, Zhao and Qin during the mid and late Warring States Period. The size of the round hole varies from the smaller one in earlier times to the bigger one later.

Wei was the first state to cast round-

• 圆形圆孔圜钱（战国 魏）

圆形圆孔圜钱面文品种较多，从左到右分别为"共""垣""共屯赤金"。

Round-holed Round Coins, State Wei (Warring States Period, 475 B.C.-221 B.C.)

Those coins have varied inscriptions, as demonstrated by these three coins which are from left to right inscribed with *Gong*, *Yuan* and *Gongtunchijin*.

　　魏国最早开始铸造圆形圆孔圜钱，品种也较多，面文有"垣""共""共屯赤金""离石""蔺""皮氏"等，也有标有重量单位"釿"字的，如"共半釿"。

　　赵国的圆形圆孔圜钱仅铸地名，不标重量单位。

　　秦国的圆形圆孔圜钱不铸地名，以"铢""两"为名称，如"铢一重一两·十二"，文字按顺时针方向列于钱面上。存世的还有文信钱、长安钱。文信是秦文信侯吕不韦丞相在河南封地所铸。

圆形方孔圜钱

　　穿孔为方形的圜钱，铸行于战国晚期，是秦、齐、燕等国的铸币。早期方孔较小，后期逐渐变

holed round coins, which are of great varieties. Inscription on those coins are 垣 (*Yuan*), 共 (*Gong*), 共屯赤金 (*Gongtunchijin*), 离石 (*Lishi*), 蔺 (*Lin*) or 皮氏 (*Pishi*), and sometimes of a weight unit measured by *Jin*, such as 共半釿 (*Gongbanjin*, half *Jin* coin of *Gong*).

　　Round-holed round coins of Zhao are inscribed with place names but without weight unit.

　　Qin round coins are not inscribed with place names. They are referred to by their units Zhu and Liang, e.g. 铢 一 重一两·十二 (Zhu Yi Zhong Yi Liang Shi'er), which are inscribed in a clockwise circle on the obverse. Among the extant coins there are the 文信 (Wenxin, title of Lü Buwei, Prime Minister of Qin) coin and 长 安 (Chang'an, name of Emperor

大。面文一般为二字或四字铭文，背文多记值、记年、记地，或铸有星纹、月纹。

秦国圜钱最初为圆形圆孔，后来逐渐演变成圆形方孔。齐国的圆形方孔圜钱则沿用刀币单位"化"，有"賹化""賹四化""賹六化"三种。燕国的圆形方孔圜钱有"一化""明（晏）化"等。

- 半两钱（战国 秦）
Ban-Liang Coin, State Qin (Warring States Period, 475 B.C.-221 B.C.)

Shihuang's brother) coin. The former was cast by order of Lü Buwei in his feoff in Henan.

Square-holed Round Coins

Round coins with a square hole were cast and circulated in States Qin, Qi and Yan in the late Warring States Period. The hole was originally smaller, and was broadened through time. The inscription is usually of two or four characters on the obverse, while on the reverse it is either inscribed the value, year or place, or patterns of the star or the moon.

Qin round coins changed from the round-holed ones to the square-holed ones. Round coins of Qi inherited the unit *Hua* of the knife-shaped coin, and have three types, namely 賹化 (*Ai Hua*), 賹四化 (*Ai Si Hua*) and 賹六化 (*Ai Liu Hua*). Coins of Yan are the 一化 (*Yi Hua*, one *Hua*) coins, the 明 (or 晏) 化 coins, etc.

- 圆形方孔圜钱（战国 燕）
Square-holed Round Coin, State Yan (Warring States Period, 475 B.C.-221 B.C.)

方孔圆钱的种类

方孔圆钱是中国古代钱币中最常见的币类。因钱文不同，分为不同的类别。

年号钱：也称"元号钱"，钱面铸有年号的钱。如"乾元重宝""太平通宝"等。

国号钱：钱面铸有国号的钱。如"大唐通宝""大宋通宝"等。

记重钱：钱文铸有重量的钱。如"半两""五铢"等。

记值钱：钱文铸有价值的钱。如"大泉五十""小泉直一"等。

记年钱：钱背铸有铸造年代的钱。

记号钱：铸有铸造地名或钱监（钱局）名称的钱。如"开元通宝"背铸"洛""兖""越"等。以月文、星文、决文、祥云等纹饰作为记号。如秦"半两"穿上星。

- 大宋通宝当拾背面（南宋）
Back Of *Dasong Tongbao Dangshi*
(Southern Song Dynasty, 1127-1279)

- 大宋通宝当拾正面（南宋）
Front Of *Dasong Tongbao Dangshi*
(Southern Song Dynasty, 1127-1279)

Various Square-holed Round Coins

Square-holed round coins are the most common type of ancient Chinese coins. They are classified into different groups according to the inscription types.

Reign Title Coins: Coins inscribed with a period name, e.g. *Qianyuan Zhongbao* and *Taiping Tongbao*.

Dynasty Title Coins: Coins of inscription containing a dynasty title, such as *Datang Tongbao* and *Dasong Tongbao*.

Weight Indicating Coins: Coins inscribed with their weight, like *Ban-Liang* and *Wu-Zhu*.

Value Indicating Coins: Coins inscribed with their value, such as *Daquan Wushi* and *Xiaoquan Zhiyi*.

Year Indicating Coins: Coins inscribed with the year of casting.

Organization / Place Name Coins: Coins inscribed with the name of the place or the mint. For example, the *Kaiyuan Tongbao* coins are inscribed on the reverse with names like 洛 (*Luo*), 兖 (*Yan*) and 越 (*Yue*) and marked by patterns of the moon, the stars, *Juewen* or clouds. The *Ban-Liang* coins of Qin are decorated with the pattern of stars.

• 大泉五十（新莽）
Daquan Wushi (Xinmang Period, 9-23)

楚国的金版

战国时期已经形成了比较完备的货币体系，主要的货币形式有布币、刀币、圜钱、蚁鼻钱四种。此外，在长江流域的楚国已经进入了黄金铸币的初级阶段。楚国拥有丰富的黄金资源，最早以黄金作为称量货币，在国间礼聘、游说诸侯、国王赠赏时使用。

楚国的黄金货币选用品相好的天然金块熔铸而成，称为"金版"。金版又称"金印子""印子金"，形状有龟背形、长方形、圆饼形等，钤有阴文印记，形似印章。印文通常排列成平行的四行分布在金版上，一印一小方，少数为圆形，若干小方构成一大方，大方有二印、四印、五印、十四印至六十印不等。

• 金版（战国 楚）
Gold Block Money, State Chu (Warring States Period, 475 B.C.-221 B.C.)

金版是一种称量货币，使用时根据需要分割成小块，称量支付，不具有金属铸币的面额价值。金版有铜、铅、泥三种质地的仿制品，泥质居多。

金版印文大多为楚国地名，有"郢爰""陈爰""鬲爰""卢金""颍""寿春""郢称""专锊"等，皆为阴文，也有一些无印文。"爰"原是重量单位，在金版中成为货币的重量单位，一爰即楚制一斤，约250克。"郢"是楚国都城，今湖北江陵纪南城。"郢爰"是楚金币中出现最早、当今出土最多的一种，因而多作为楚国黄金货币的代表。

楚金版成色极佳，含金量通常在96%以上，一直被使用到西汉初年，入汉后见马蹄形、铤状等黄金铸币。

- "郢称"金版（战国 楚）
Gold Block Money Inscribed with 郢称 (*Yingcheng*), State Chu (Warring States Period, 475 B.C.-221 B.C.)

Gold Block Money of the State Chu

The money system was rather complete during the Warring States Period, and the major currency were the *Bu* coins, knife-shaped coins, round coins and the ant-nose coins. Meanwhile, the State of Chu along the Yangtze River, which was abundant in gold, had entered the primary stage of gold block casting. Chu was the first to use gold as money valued by weight, employed in engaging able persons from other states, lobbying feudal princes of other states or when the King granted a reward.

Chu gold block money, also called the intaglio gold block, was cast by melting and remolding selected good-looking natural gold blocks. A cast block may be of the shape of a turtle shell, an oblong cube or a round plate, with an intaglioed inscription like that on a stamp. Usually the inscription is arranged into four parallel rows of small squares or, in a few cases, rounds, of characters, many small squares forming a big square. Each big square may contain two to sixty small squares.

A gold block, as a kind of money valued by weight instead of by face value as were the metallic coins, was cut into small blocks of appointed weight when used. Mimics of the gold block were made of copper, lead and clay, the last being the most in number.

The inscription is often the combination of a place name of Chu such as *Yingyuan, Chenyuan, Geyuan, Lujin, Ying, Shouchun, Yingcheng, Zhuanlüe*, etc., all of which are carved in intaglio. Some of them don't have the inscriptions. The *Yuan* is originally a weight unit and then is used as the currency weight unit in gold block. 1 *Yuan* equals to 1 *Jin* of the State Chu, approx. 250 g. Ying was the capital city of the State Chu, which is the present Jinan Town of Jiangling, Hubei Province. *Yingyuan* gold block was the earliest of the State Chu's gold blocks, and also the greatest in number of its kind unearthed so far. For such reasons, it is taken as the representative of the State Chu's gold block money.

The gold blocks of the State Chu are of high quality alloy, usually containing over 96% gold. They were in use till the early Western Han Dynasty, when gold blocks shaped like a horseshoe or a boat appeared.

- "专钘"金版（战国 楚）
  Gold Block Inscribed with 专钘 (*Zhuanlüe*), State Chu (Warring States Period, 475 B.C.-221 B.C.)

> 秦汉钱币

半两钱

秦朝在战国时期秦国圆形方孔钱的基础上，将半两钱作为全国通用的法定货币。秦半两钱形制为圆形方孔，无内外郭，背平无文。"半两"既是钱文，也是记重。"半""两"二字布局严谨，高挺刚健，分列于方孔左右，通常是右"半"左"两"；半两钱重半两，即12铢（中国古代规定一两为24铢）。

秦半两钱的标准不高，钱肉或厚或薄，边缘不够光滑，钱体欠圆，是比较粗糙的货币。钱文书体用小篆，方中有圆。其质地为青铜，但事实上铜约占70%，其余金属成分为铅、锡等。

汉初，高祖刘邦沿用秦朝的货

> Currencies of the Qin Dynasty (221 B.C.-206 B.C.) and Han Dynasty (206 B.C.-220 A.D.)

Ban-Liang Coins

Following the square-holed round coin circulated in the State Qin during the Warring States Period, Qin Dynasty issued the *Ban-Liang* (*Ban-Liang* means half a *Liang*; *Liang* was the ancient Chinese weight unit, consisting of 24 *Zhu*, and was the equivalent of about 16 grams) coin as the legal currency circulating around the country. *Ban-Liang* is also a round coin with a square hole in the middle, but neither the round edge nor the square edge is outlined. The reverse is at since there is no inscription on it. *Ban-Liang* refers to both the value and the weight of the coin. The two characters 半 (*Ban*) and 两 (*Liang*) on the two sides of the square hole (usually *Ban*

• 半两钱（秦）
Ban-Liang Coin (Qin Dynasty, 221 B.C.-206 B.C.)

on the right while *Liang* on the left) look solemn, bold and vigorous. The *Ban-Liang* coin weighs half Liang, which is 12 *Zhu* (8 g).

The *Ban-Liangs* in the Qin Dynasty are roughly made as they are not equal in thickness, their edges are not smooth, and their shapes not round. The inscriptions on the coins are carved in small seal style that rendered the characters square with circular strokes. The coins are cast mainly in bronze which takes 70% of the total weight, and the other components are metals like lead and tin.

币制度，所铸的钱币仍称作"半两"。因连年战争，生产萎缩，货币重量不断减轻。汉高祖令民间私

半两钱的重量

半两钱虽都写有"半两"，史书上也说"重如其文"，但其实际的重量却差许多。司马迁在《史记·平准书》中指出："秦汉两代铸行的半两钱，轻重无常。"半两钱的重量变化无常不是偶然的现象，而是由以下几个因素造成的：

首先，秦朝时期钱范多为泥陶范，其伸缩性大，不能保证重量一致，也容易造成形状不一。

其次，不同统治者对半两的规定不同。秦半两以12铢为半两；西汉吕后以8铢为半两；汉文帝又以4铢为半两。

最后，秦末汉初，民间私铸半两钱，随意减轻重量，铸造的半两轻如榆荚，重量自然不足。

Weight of *Ban-Liang* Coin

Despite the fact that *Ban-Liang* is inscribed on the coin, and that "it weighed as it indicates" according to history records, the *Ban-Liang* coin actually does not weigh as it indicates. Sima Qian wrote in *Records of the Grand Historian: Equalization* that the weights of the *Ban-Liang* coins cast in the Qin Dynasty and the Han Dynasty were not always the same. It was no accident that the weight of the *Ban-Liang* coin varied from time to time as it was affected by the following factors:

Firstly, the coin moulds were mostly made of clay, a flexible material which probably caused various weights and shapes of the coins.

Secondly, different emperors set different standards for *Ban-Liang* coins. In the Qin Dynasty, *Ban-Liang* weighed 12 *Zhu*, and was reduced to 8 *Zhu* during the reign of Queen Lü in the Western Han Dynasty, and to 4 *Zhu* when Emperor Wen of Han reigned over the country.

Finally, during the late Qin Dynasty and the early Han Dynasty, people who privately cast *Ban-Liang* reduced the weight without restriction. As a result, those coins were as light as the elm seeds, far from weighing *Ban-Liang*.

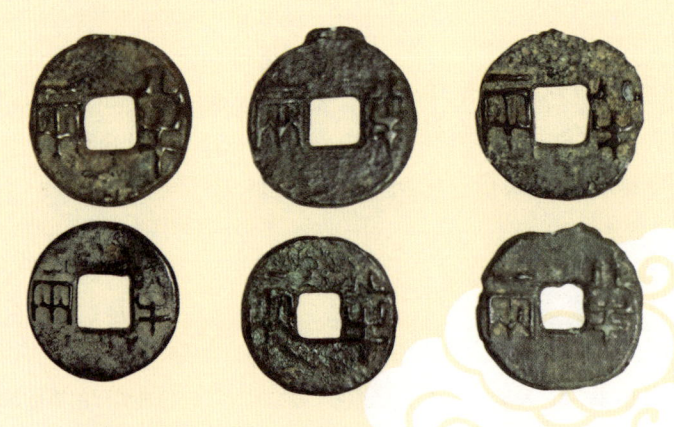

- 半两钱（秦）
Ban-Liang Coins (Qin Dynasty, 221 B.C.-206 B.C.)

铸钱，导致钱体轻薄，有的轻至一铢以下，即"榆荚钱"。

高后二年（前186年），因秦半两太重，榆荚半两太轻，吕后下令新铸半两钱，重8铢，俗称"八铢半两"。八铢半两铸作精整，形

In the beginning of the Han Dynasty, Emperor Gaozu of Han (Liu Bang) still called the coins *Ban-Liang*, succeeding to the coinage system in the Qin Dynasty. The weight of the coins, however, was continuously reduced due to economic downturn caused by years of war.

榆荚钱（西汉）
Yujia Coins (Western Han Dynasty, 206 B.C.-25 A.D.)

大肉薄，穿孔大小基本一致，钱文扁平，是汉半两中最大的钱币。然而，八铢半两流通不久，多被商人贮藏，或私自熔化，减轻重量改铸成较小的榆荚钱以牟取利益。

高后六年（前182年），在军费开支大增的情况下，又推行货币减重，铸造"五分钱"。五分钱即半两的五分之一，仅重2.4铢，穿孔较大，钱文亦为"半两"，属于一种官方所铸的榆荚钱。

汉文帝五年（前175年），又铸行"四铢半两"，形体小，穿孔小，内外无郭，周缘整齐，钱文"半两"二字为小篆，文字规整，笔画方折。这种半两钱流通至汉武帝元狩四年（前119年）。

Liu Bang allowed the people to cast coins, which also led to the reduction of the weight of the coins. Some coins, weighing less than 1 *Zhu*, were thus known as *Yujia* (the elm seed) coins.

In the 2nd year of the Gaohou Period (186 B.C.), as the *Ban-Liang* of the Qin Dynasty was too heavy while *Yujia* was too light, Queen Lü ordered to recast *Ban-Liang* weighing 8 *Zhu*, known as *Bazhu Ban-Liang*. Cast with neat appearance and precise measure, *Bazhu Ban-Liang* is large (the largest among all types of *Ban-Liang* coins in the Han Dynasty), thin, and inscribed with at characters, and the holes of different coins are almost of the same size. Soon after *Bazhu Ban-Liang* issued, however, it was stocked up, or melted in secret and recast into lighter

Yujia coins by merchants who attempted to gain improper profits.

In the 6th year of the Gaohou Period (182 B.C.), because of a huge increase in military expenditure, Queen Lü reduced the weight of the coins and cast a new type of coin, *Wufen* coin, an officially cast *Yujia* coin. Wufen, i.e., half of *Ban-Liang*, weighed only 2.4 *Zhu*. The hole in the middle is larger, yet the characters on the coin remain 半两 (*Ban-Liang*).

In the 5th year of the reign of the Emperor Wen of Han (175 B.C.), a coin called *Sizhu Ban-Liang* was issued. It is small, and the hole is small, too. The edges are neat and there is no outline. The characters *Ban-Liang*, inscribed in the small seal style appear neat. *Sizhu Ban-Liang* had been circulating until the 4th year of the Yuanshou Period (119 B.C.).

Wu-Zhu Coins

In the 5th year of the Yuanshou Period (118 B.C.), Emperor Wu of Han reformed the coinage system. He forbade people to cast coins in private, and abolished *Ban-Liang* coins which had been used since the Qin Dynasty, and started to cast *Wu-Zhu* coins. From then on, this kind of coin had been produced by the succeeding

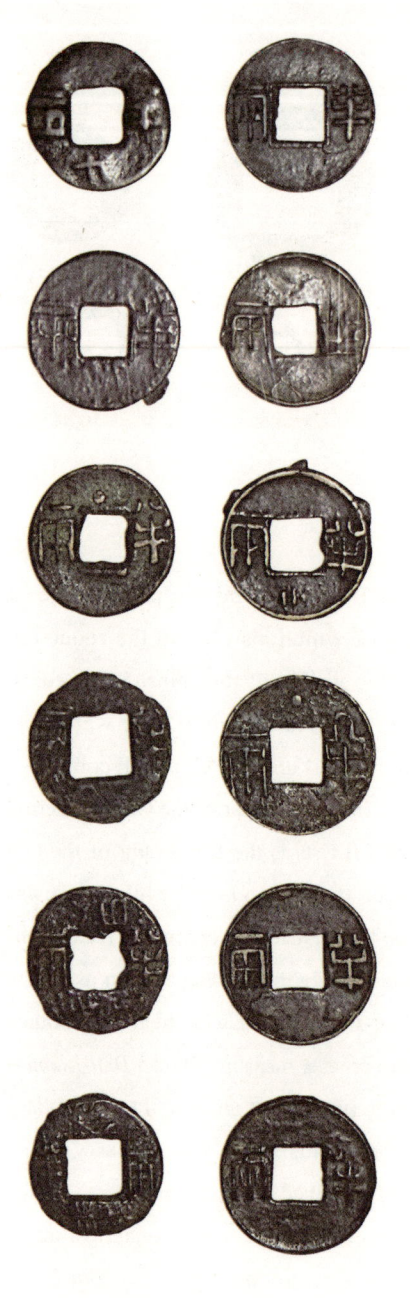

• 四铢半两钱（西汉）
Sizhu Ban-Liang Coins (Western Han Dynasty, 206 B.C.-25 A.D.)

五铢钱

元狩五年（前118年），汉武帝下令禁止私人铸钱，实行币制改革，废除自秦以来一直流通的半两钱，始铸五铢钱。此后，西汉的武、昭、宣、元、成、哀、平各帝，均有铸造五铢钱。各帝铸造的五铢钱形制与风格基本一致，方孔圆钱，大小、轻重适宜，铜色凝重，轮廓整齐，铸有内外郭。五铢钱的重铢，钱文"五铢"端庄秀雅，为篆书，横读。

emperors of Western Han Dynasty, Emperor Zhao, Emperor Xuan, Emperor Yuan, Emperor Cheng, Emperor Ai, and Emperor Ping. The *Wu-Zhu* coins cast in the reign of these emperors are alike in style. They are round with a square hole, with suitable sizes and weights, heavy color of copper, neat profiles, and outlines along inside and outside edges. The weight mark of this coin, *Wu-Zhu*, read right to left, is elegantly carved in seal style.

The shapes, sizes, materials, and weights of coins were variable before

---

三铢钱

元狩四年（前119年），汉武帝铸行"三铢钱"。三铢钱面文"三铢"，从右往左横读，背平无郭。三铢钱是中国钱币史上流通时间最短的钱币，仅铸行了几个月，就因钱轻被汉武帝停铸。

San-Zhu Coins

In the 4th year of the Yuanshou Period (119 B.C.), Emperor Wu of Han issued *San-Zhu* coin (the coin that weighs three *Zhu*). The characters on the coin, 三铢, are read from the right, and there is no rim on the reverse. Circulating only for several months before it was banned, *San-Zhu* coin was one that existed for the shortest time in the history of Chinese coinage.

- 三铢钱（西汉）
  San-Zhu Coins (Western Han Dynasty, 206 B.C.-25 A.D.)

• 五铢钱（汉）

Wu-Zhu Coins (Han Dynasty, 206 B.C.-220 A.D.)

在铸行五铢钱以前，钱币的形制、大小、材质、重量都不统一，使用很不方便。五铢钱以其精美的做工、携带的便利，使这种状况大为改观，在汉代疆域内广为流行，成为当时统一的货币。从汉武帝到汉平帝元始三年（3年）的120年内，共铸造五铢钱280亿枚。此后，一直到唐初武德四年（621年）更行"开元通宝"、废五铢钱为止，均有铸造五铢钱。

西汉五铢钱以郡国五铢、赤仄五铢和上林三官五铢最有代表性。

郡国五铢：元狩五年（前118年），汉武帝令各郡国铸行五铢

Wu-Zhu coin was cast. As a result, there had been troubles in the circulation of the coins. *Wu-Zhu* coin, which was exquisite and convenient to carry, was improved and became the unified currency within the territory of the Han Dynasty. 28 billion *Wu-Zhu* coins were produced over 120 years, that is, from the reign of Emperor Wu to the 3rd year of the Yuanshi Period (3). Even after that, *Wu-Zhu* coins were still produced until 621, the 4th year of the Wude Period (618-626), when *Kaiyuan Tongbao* was issued and *Wu-Zhu* was abolished.

Junguo Wu-Zhu, *Chize Wu-Zhu*, and *Shanglin Sanguan Wu-Zhu* were the most representative *Wu-Zhu* coins in the Western Han Dynasty.

Junguo Wu-Zhu: In the 5th year of the Yuanshou Period (118 B.C.), Emperor Wu of the Han Dynasty ordered all prefectural states to produce *Wu-Zhu* coin, which was known as *Junguo Wu-Zhu* in history. The crafts of the coins were uneven and the characters on the coins unregulated, since most *Junguo Wu-Zhu* coins were not officially cast.

Chize Wu-Zhu: In the 2nd year of the Yuanding Period (115 B.C.), Emperor Wu of the Han Dynasty requested the mints in the capital to produce *Chize*

钱，史称"郡国五铢"。由于"郡国五铢"多为私铸，铸造工艺优劣不一，钱文书体不规范。

赤仄五铢：元鼎二年（前115年），汉武帝命京师铸"赤仄五铢"。赤仄五铢属赋官用钱，非流通钱币，一枚赤仄五铢当五枚郡国五铢，是汉武帝敛取地方财物的产物。其含铜量高，铸造规矩，周郭经锉磨后，显出赤色。

上林三官五铢：元鼎四年（前113年），汉武帝废止"郡国五铢"

• 郡国五铢（西汉）
Junguo Wu-Zhu Coins (Western Han Dynasty, 206 B.C.-25 A.D.)

• 五铢叠铸铜制范盒（西汉）
Overlapping Cast Copper Model Case of Wu-Zhu Coin (Western Han Dynasty, 206 B.C.-25 A.D.)

(referring to the red or shining edge of the coin) *Wu-Zhu* coins. This type of coin was cast as the government official grants instead of being circulated. With one worth five *Junguo Wu-Zhu* coins, *Chize Wu-Zhu* was produced to meet Emperor Wu's need of amassing wealth from the prefectural states. This coin has a large amount of red copper and is cast according to strict regulation. The color red will show itself if the edge of the coin is filed smooth.

Shanglin Sanguan Wu-Zhu: In the 4th year of the Yuanding Period (113 B.C.), Emperor Wu of the Han Dynasty abolished *Junguo Wu-Zhu* and *Chize Wu-Zhu*, and ordered *Shanglin Sanguan* (The Three Offices of *Shanglin* Park, the Office of Coinage, the Office of Sorting Copper, and the Office of Price

和"赤仄五铢",令上林三官铸行五铢钱,把铸币权收归中央,史称"上林三官五铢"。其铸工精美,钱文规范统一,笔画清晰工整,周郭圆润。

Equalisation) to produce coins which were known as *Shanglin Sanguan Wu-Zhu* coins. The coins are exquisite. The characters on the coin are regulated and their strokes are neat. The edges of the coins are smooth.

王莽币制改革

汉元帝时,外戚王莽篡权夺位,改国号为"新",史称"新莽"。王莽在篡位前后一共进行了四次币制改革,托古改制,模仿战国钱币,铸造了刀币、泉币、布币等"六名二十八品(形制)"货币。

这四次币制改革,扰乱了民心,加上与匈奴连年战争,引发财政恐慌,新莽政权很快走向了覆灭。虽然王莽的币制改革均以失败告终,但其铸币铸造工整,形制独特,书法俊美,对中国古代货币文化产生了深远的影响。

新莽钱币无论从种类、面额还是钱文书体上,都超越古代任何一位帝王所铸的钱币。王莽因此被清代钱币学家誉为"古今第一铸钱能手"。

Wang Mang's Currency Reforms

Wang Mang, a relative on the maternal side of the emperor, usurped the throne of Emperor Yuan of Han, and founded the Xin Dynasty, known as Xinmang. He held four currency reforms around his usurpation. Following the coinage system of Warring States Period, he asked to cast currency made of six types of materials and, considering different materials, shapes and values, there were twenty-eight kinds of coins in total, such as knife-shaped coins, *Quan* coins, and *Bu* coins.

The Xinmang Regime was overthrown soon. Its overthrow was attributed to the currency reforms which disturbed people's peaceful life and the financial crisis caused by the wars with the Hun for years. Although the currency reforms introduced by Wang Mang ended in failure, they were seminal for ancient Chinese coinage culture with the neatness of the crafts, the uniqueness of the forms, and the elegance of the characters on the coins.

The coins made during Xinmang surpassed all the coins made by previous emperors in terms of its types, denomination, and the calligraphy of the characters on the coins. Wang Mang was therefore called "the best coin maker in history" by the numismatists in the Qing Dynasty.

第一次币制改革

居摄二年（7年），王莽篡位前，新铸大额错刀、契刀、大泉，强令与五铢钱比价并行。错刀、契刀、大泉属于大面额铸币，是靠行政命令强力推行的虚币值钱。

The First Currency Reform

In the 2nd year of the Jushe Period (7), Wang Mang introduced new types of money such as *Cuo* knife-shaped coin of large bill, *Qi* knife-shaped coin, *Daquan*, and they were allowed to be exchanged with *Wu-Zhu* coin. *Cuo* knife-shaped coin, *Qi* knife-shaped coin, and *Daquan*, although having large denomination set by the government, were not as valuable as their denominations suggested.

- **错刀（新莽）**

错刀，又叫"金错刀""一刀平五千"，一枚错刀比价五千枚五铢钱。环首刀身，青铜质，钱穿上下有用黄金错成的阴文"一刀"二字，刀身阳文篆书"平五千"三字。钱文丰满，郭宽肉厚，铸造精美。

Cuo Knife-shaped Coin (Xinmang Period, 9-23)

Cuo knife-shaped coin, or the "Gold *Cuo* knife-shaped coin", *Yidao Pingwuqian* (the coin worth five thousand), is the coin that equaled 5,000 *Wu-Zhu* coins. It has a round head and a long body, and is cast in bronze. Characters "一" (*Yi*) and "刀" (*Dao*) are filed in intaglio with gold respectively above and under the hole in the middle of the round head, and "平五千" (*Pingwuqian*) are inscribed in relief on the body. The coin looks exquisite and beautiful with its round and full characters, wide edges, and thick body.

- **契刀（新莽）**

契刀，又名"契刀五百"，一枚契刀比价五百枚五铢钱。形制与错刀相似，钱文不同。方孔圆钱的钱穿左右铸有阳文"契刀"二字，刀部铸有阳文"五百"二字。

Qi Knife-shaped Coin (Xinmang Period, 9-23)

Qi knife-shaped coin, or *Qidao Wubai* (the coin worth five hundred), is the coin that equaled 500 *Wu-Zhu* coins. It looks like *Cuo* knife-shaped coin but valued less. The characters "契刀" (*Qidao*) are inscribed in relief on the two sides of the square hole, while "五百" (*Wubai*) are on the body.

第二次币制改革

始建国元年（9年），废错刀、契刀和五铢钱，新铸小泉，与原有大泉并行。王莽强行通用小钱，破坏了汉武帝以来专由上林三官铸钱的制度，使币制更加混乱。

The Second Currency Reform

In 9, *Cuo* knife-shaped coin, *Qi* knife-shaped coin and *Wu-Zhu* coin were abolished, and coin with small value was issued circulating with *Daquan*, the coin that was issued in the first reform. As he forced to produce coins with less value, Wang Mang broke the currency system applied since Emperor Wu of the Han Dynasty that coins were cast only by *Shanglin Sanguan*, and therefore brought more troubles to the currency system.

- **大泉五十（新莽）**

泉币仿先秦圆形方孔圜钱铸造，内外有郭，铸有记名、记值铭文，最主要的是泉货六品。泉货六品又称"六泉"，有小泉直一、么泉一十、幼泉二十、中泉三十、壮泉四十、大泉五十，形制相同，制作精美，大小轻重依次递增，其中大泉和小泉数量最多，其余则很少见。

Daquan Wushi (Xinmang Period, 9-23)

Quan coins modeled after the square-holed circular coin cast in the Qin Dynasty, have outlines along both the inside and outside edges and characters suggesting the name and value of the coin. The main types of *Quan* coins are the Six Coins, including *Xiaoquan Zhiyi*, *Yaoquan Yishi*, *Youquan Ershi*, *Zhongquan Sanshi*, *Zhuangquan Sishi*, and *Daquan Wushi*. The Six Coins are cast exquisitely and share the same design, while their sizes and weights ascend from *Xiaoquan Zhiyi* to *Daquan Wushi*. *Daquan* and *Xiaoquan* are the most commonly seen coins, while others are rare.

第三次币制改革

始建国二年（10年），推行"宝货制"。《汉书·食货志》中说："凡宝货，五物、六名、二十八品。"五物指金、银、铜、龟、贝五种质地的币材；六名指金货、银货、龟货、贝货、泉货和布货六大钱币类型；二十八品是不同形制不同单位的二十八品钱币，即金货一品、银货二品、龟货四品、贝货五品、泉货六品和布货十品。

其中泉货六品和布货十品是铜铸币。布货十品又称"十布"，有小布一百、么布二百、幼布三百、序布四百、差布五百、中布六百、壮布七百、第布八百、次布九百、大布黄千。布货十品模仿战国平首布形态，布首铸一圆孔，圆孔与币周均有郭；布面中部自首至裆铸一道直线，或通首顶部，或通至首部圆孔，直线两侧为阳文篆书钱文，字体道劲有力，上下右左读。

宝货制名目繁多，币值悬殊，通行不久就废止了。

The Third Currency Reform

In 10, Wang Mang implemented the *Baohuo* System. It is said in the *Book of Han: Treatise on Food and Money* that "The Five *Wus*, The Six *Mings*, and The Twenty-Eight *Pins* can be called *Bao Huo*." The Five *Wus* refer to the five types of materials of which the coins are made, gold, silver, copper, tortoise shell, and cowries. The Six *Mings* refer to the six types of coins, *Jinhuo, Yinhuo, Guihuo, Beihuo, Quanhuo* and *Buhuo*. The Twenty-Eight Pins refer to the twenty-eight kinds of coins classified according to their differences in design and denomination, including *Jinhuo Yipin, Yinhuo Erpin, Guihuo Sipin, Beihuo Wupin, Quanhuo Liupin, Buhuo Shipin*,etc.

Quanhuo Liupin and *Buhuo Shipin* are made of copper. *Buhuo Shipin*, or *Shibu*, included *Xiaobu Yibai, Yaobu Erbai, Youbu Sanbai, Xubu Sibai, Chabu Wubai, Zhongbu Liubai, Zhuangbu Qibai, Dibu Babai, Cibu Jiubai* and *Dabu Huangqian*. Modeled upon the design of the flat-headed *Bu* coin in the Warring States Period, *Buhuo Shipin* has a round hole on the head, and both the edge of the hole and the outer rim of the coin are outlined. In the middle of the coin body, there is a straight line going from either the top of the head or the hole down to the crutch. The characters, read from above and from right, are inscribed vigorously in relief on the two sides of the straight line.

Baohuo System was so complex and the values of different types of coins varied so much that it was abolished soon after implemented.

第四次币制改革

天凤元年（14年），废大泉、小泉，铸行货布、货泉。以一货布比价二十五货泉流通，结果引起私铸者私自铸造，使币制更加混乱。

- 货布（新莽）

货布仿战国时期平首方足布的形态，布首铸一圆孔，首上圆孔及布身均有周郭，货布铸造精美，轮郭纤细。直线两侧为阳文钱文"货布"二字，悬针篆（笔划上粗下细，如悬着的一根针），书法俊逸，右左读。货布与货泉并行流通。一货布比价二十五货泉。

Huobu (Xinmang Period, 9-23)

Modeled upon the flat-headed square foot *Bu* coin in the Warring Stated Period, *Huobu* has a round hole on the head, and both the hole and the edge of the body are outlined. The coin is exquisite with its slender outlines. In the middle of the body, from the hole down to the crutch there goes a straight line, on the two sides of which the handsome characters "货布" (*Huobu*, reading from right) are inscribed in relief in the style of suspending needle seal (a seal style that makes the stroke thick above while thin below, looking like a suspending needle). Both *Huobu* and *Huoquan* were circulated in the market, with one *Huobu* worth twenty-five *Huoquan*.

The Fourth Currency Reform

In the 1st year of the Tianfeng Period (14), *Daquan* and *Xiaoquan* were abolished, while *Huobu* and *Huoquan* were issued. With one *Huobu* worth twenty-five *Huoquan*, this rate of exchange brought more troubles to the currency system since many people began to cast coins in private.

- **货泉（新莽）**

  货泉为圆形方孔，面背肉好皆有周郭。面文阳文"货泉"二字，悬针篆，右左读，书法俊美，竖笔上粗下细，住笔纤细如针。"泉"字直竖中断，为莽钱独有的特色。

  Huoquan (Xinmang Period, 9-23)

  Huoquan is a kind of round coin with a square hole in the middle, with inner and outer rims on the obverse and the reverse. The handsome characters "货泉" (*Huoquan*), read right to left, are inscribed in relief in the style of the suspending needle seal. The vertical stroke becomes thinner when it goes down, and finally is slender as a needle where it stops. There is a break in the middle of the character "泉" (*Quan*), which is a unique feature of the coins made by Wang Mang.

西汉黄金货币

　　西汉法定的黄金货币有金饼、马蹄金、麟趾金、金五铢等，属于称量货币，不是铸币。西汉的黄金货币需要称量交易，重量比较规范，很少被切割。其中金饼和马蹄金的底部还标有重量。

　　汉代盛行冥钱，在湖南出土的西汉初期墓中常有一种泥质金版，印文"郢爰""郢孚""郢""两""称"等字，有的印文刻有阳文"金""千金千两"等字。有的泥质金版还涂有一层象征黄金的黄粉或金粉。

The Gold Currencies in the Western Han Dynasty

The officially cast gold currencies in the Western Han Dynasty included the Gold Plate, the Horseshoe-shaped Gold, the Kylinshoe-shaped Gold, the Gold *Wu-Zhu*, etc. Valued by weight instead of by the denomination as were the minted coins, the gold currencies in the Western Han

Dynasty weighed stably as they were seldom cut away. There are marks of weight at the bottom of the Gold Plate and the Horseshoe-shaped Gold.

The false money cast for the dead was popular in the Han Dynasty. A false gold currency made of earth is often excavated from tombs of the beginning period of the Western Han Dynasty in Hunan. Characters such as *Yingyuan, Yinglüe, Ying, Liang, Cheng*, etc., or " 金 " (*Jin*, gold), " 千金千两 " (*Qianjin Qianliang*, a thousand gold and a thousand *Liang*) in relief. To make the dead believe that these currencies were made of real gold, people sometimes spread yellow or golden powders on the surface of the money.

• 金饼（西汉）

金饼呈圆形饼状，形如熟透了的柿子，故又称"柿子金"。正背面皆实而不空，有大、小两种形制。大金饼重约250克，相当于西汉一斤左右；小金饼重15.1～17.99克，相当于西汉一两左右。金饼上往往刻有文字、数字或记重。

Gold Plate(Western Han Dynasty, 206 B.C.-25 A.D.)

Taking the shape of a round cake and meanwhile like a ripe persimmon, the gold plate is therefore called the "Gold Persimmon" as well, and it is not hollow on either the obverse or the reverse. There are two kinds of gold plate classified according to their sizes. The large gold plate weighs about 250 grams, roughly equal to a Jin in the Western Han Dynasty; while the small one weighs from 15.1 to 17.99 grams, about 1 *Liang* at that time. There are usually characters, numbers or remarks of the weight on the gold plates.

• 马蹄金（西汉）

马蹄金形如马蹄，底大口小，正面呈椭圆形，背面中空，周壁向上收缩成斜面。重量多在250克左右，个别重达460余克。早在战国末期就已出现马蹄金，西汉曾广泛使用。

Horseshoe-shaped Gold (Western Han Dynasty, 206 B.C.-25 A.D.)

The horseshoe-shaped gold looks like a horse's hoof. It is large at the bottom and small on the top, elliptical on the obverse and hollow on the reverse, and the body is like a slope as its circumference gets smaller from the bottom to the top. Most horseshoe-shaped gold weighed 250 grams also, and a few of them weighed as heavy as over 460 grams. The horseshoe-shaped gold appeared in as early as the end of the Warring States Period and was popular in the Western Han Dynasty.

- 麟趾金（西汉）

  麟为传说中的神兽，麟趾为圆，以麟趾命名黄金，表示祥瑞之意。麟趾金形如圆足兽蹄，底大口小，正面呈圆形，或近似圆，背面中空，周壁向上斜收。重量约为250克。

  Kylinshoe-shaped Gold (Western Han Dynasty, 206 B.C.-25 A.D.)

  Kylin was the divine beast in ancient Chinese legend. The gold currency is named after the hoof of kylin, which is round, so as to indicate auspice. The kylinshoe-shaped gold, looking like the round hoof of kylin, is large at the bottom and small on the top, round or nearly round on the obverse and hollow on the reverse, and the profile of the body looks like a slope. It weighs 250 grams or so.

- 金五铢（西汉）

  金五铢形态规范，铸造精细，周缘有郭，穿上有一横，面文篆书"五铢"二字。金五铢是西汉大量使用的黄金货币。

  Gold *Wu-Zhu* Coin (Western Han Dynasty, 206 B.C.-25 A.D.)

  A widely used gold currency in the Western Han Dynasty, the gold *Wu-Zhu* is neatly shaped and exquisitely cast, with outlines along the edge, a horizontal line above the hole, and characters 五铢 (*Wu-Zhu*) on the surface.

东汉建武十六年（40年）铸造五铢钱，称为"建武五铢"，制作精致，铜色略红，有外郭。钱文篆书"五铢"二字，笔画较细，文字书体规范，重量比西汉五铢钱轻。有的钱

In the 16th year of the Jianwu Periof (40) of the Eastern Han Dynasty (25-220), a *Wu-Zhu* coin known as *Jianwu Wu-Zhu* was issued. *Jianqu Wu-Zhu*, lighter than the *Wu-Zhu* in the Western Han Dynasty, is exquisitely made, the

• 建武五铢（东汉）
Jianwu Wu-Zhu (Eastern Han Dynasty, 25-220)

上标记有星纹、横道、竖纹等纹饰。

在汉武帝之后，通货膨胀，开始流行磨边五铢，又称"磨边钱"，就是磨去外郭边缘的五铢钱。磨边的目的，在于取镕，铸造更多的新钱。磨边的方法是用一根方形木棍或金属方棍穿进圆形钱的孔，一次约穿百枚或更多，固定好两端后，在砺上打磨钱币的轮郭。磨边使五铢钱大幅度减重。

还有一种剪边五铢，又称"对文五铢"，其外郭连同部分钱肉被剪凿或磨去，只留下内圈，钱径因凿具大小不一，差异较大。钱文"五铢"往往都各剩半边，边缘有冲截痕迹，较为粗糙。

color of the copper is slightly red, and there is outline along the outside edge. The characters "五 铢" (*Wu-Zhu*) are inscribed in regulated seal style with slender stokes. There are ornaments such as stars, horizontal lines and vertical lines on some coins.

After the reign of Emperor Wu of the Han Dynasty, the edge-ground *Wu-Zhu*, or the edge-ground coin, which is the *Wu-Zhu* coin with its outline of the outside edge rubbed, became popular due to the inflation. People rubbed off the outline in order to get extra materials for casting more coins. To grind the outline, a square wood or metal stick was firstly to be put through the holes of the round coins, usually about a hundred coins or more. Then, the stick was prepared to grind when its two ends were fixed. Grinding caused *Wu-Zhu's* huge reduction in weight.

There was an edge-chiseled *Wu-Zhu*, or *Duiwen Wu-Zhu*, whose outline of the outer edge as well as some parts of the body was chiseled or ground, with the inner circle left. As the sizes of the chiselers varied from each other, the diameters of the chiseled coins were different. In addition, the characters "五" (*Wu*) and "铢" (*Zhu*) often remained

董卓攻入长安，取铜人、铜台等熔铸无文小钱，钱形小而薄，制作粗劣，没有钱文和轮郭。此钱铸行以后，物价飞涨，钱货不行，东汉王朝形存实亡。

in half, with the uneven edges showing they had been chiseled.

Dong Zhuo melted the copper statues to cast small coins without characters after he captured Chang'an. These coins, without characters or outlines, were small, thin and roughly made. The commodity price rose rapidly after this coin was cast, and the currency condition went from bad to worse. By that time, the Eastern Han Dynasty had been on the rocks.

- **四出五铢拓本（西汉）**

自背穿郭的四角各铸出一道阳文斜线和周郭相连，称四出纹，用来和旧钱相区别。四出五铢钱被时人当做天下四方大乱的预兆。

The Rubbing Edition of *Sichu Wu-Zhu* (Western Han Dynasty, 206 B.C.-25 A.D.)

On the back of *Sichu Wu-Zhu*, there were four diagonals in relief spreading from the four corners of the square hole and joining the outline of the outer edge. These diagonals are called Sichu design, used to distinguish the coin from the previous coins. *Sichu Wu-Zhu* was believed by people at that time as the omen of the turbulence of the country.

- **綖环五铢拓本**

五铢钱的内圈被剪去或冲凿掉，一分为二，所剩边缘，呈环状，即为"綖环五铢"。钱形大小、轻重因凿具大小不一而不同，钱文"五铢"二字多不全，有的只剩一半或1/3的文字。

Rubbing Edition of *Yanhuan* (Fringe) *Wu-Zhu*

With the middle of *Wu-Zhu* chiseled to make two coins, the remained outside fringe was called *Yanhuan Wu-Zhu*. The sizes and weights vary with the sizes of the chiselers. The characters "五" (*Wu*) and "铢" (*Zhu*) were mostly incomplete, with half or one third left on the coin.

三国两晋南北朝钱币

三国钱币

三国时期，政治上处于曹魏、蜀汉、东吴三个政权的分裂对峙之中，各个政权自铸钱币，颁行币制。

曹魏钱币

公元220年曹丕称帝，建立曹魏政权，初期曾一度废钱不用，民间以谷帛交易，后铸造了"文帝五铢"和"明帝五铢"。

文帝五铢：黄初二年（221年）三月，魏文帝复铸的五铢钱形同汉制，钱体稍小于汉五铢，制作粗劣，轮郭浅平。钱文模糊，外郭压"五"又压"铢"，有星点、横画或竖画。同年十月即废止，恢复"以谷帛为市"的局面。

明帝五铢：太和元年（227

Currencies of the Three Kingdoms Period, the Western and Eastern Jin Dynasties, and the Southern and Northern Dynasties (220-589)

Coins of the Three Kingdoms Period (220-280)

The Three Kingdoms Period was an era of disunity under control of the tripartite rival regimes, Wei (or Cao-Wei) (220-265), Shu (or Shu-Han) (221-263) and Wu (or Sun-Wu) (222-280). Each Kingdom cast its own coins and had its own monetary system.

Coins of Cao-Wei

When Cao Pi proclaimed himself emperor and founded the State of Wei in 220, transaction by money was once forbidden, and people bartered grain or silk fabrics for goods. Later, coins

• 文帝五铢（三国 魏）
Wendi Wu-Zhu, Kingdom of Wei (Three Kingdoms Period, 220-280)

年），明帝复铸五铢钱。钱形厚重，铸作精细，轮廓明晰，犹似东汉五铢钱。面文"五铢"二字，清楚肥硕。明帝五铢一直沿用到西晋。

蜀汉钱币

蜀汉地处西南边陲，民寡国弱，又承受着巨大的军费开支，铸行的钱币均为大钱，较为重要的有"直百五铢""直百小钱""蜀五铢"三种五铢钱。

直百五铢：铸造于建安十九年（214年）刘备初至成都时。"直百"意为值百，一枚可当一百枚五铢钱使用。直百五铢形体较大，钱文为"直百五铢"四字，背面模铸阳文记地名"为"字，是目前发现的最早的记地名方孔圆钱。

直百小钱：蜀汉后期连年用

inscribed with *Wendi Wu-Zhu* and *Mingdi Wu-Zhu* were cast for use.

Wendi Wu-Zhu: It was cast under authorization of Emperor Wen of the Wei in March, 221. They resemble *Wu-Zhu* of the Han Dynasty in shape, but are smaller and more roughly manufactured, with a slightly raised rim. The inscription is vague, with the outer rim overlapping the characters *Wu* and *Zhu*, and accompanied by stars and horizontal or vertical lines. This currency was soon abolished in October, when barter by grain and silk was restored.

Mingdi Wu-Zhu: It was cast under the order of Emperor Ming in 227. They are thick and heavy, exquisitely cast with a clear rim, similar to the *Wu-Zhu* of the Eastern Han Dynasty. The characters 五铢 are clearly inscribed in a full shape. *Mingdi Wu-Zhu* was in use until the Western Jin Dynasty (265-317).

Coins of Shu-Han

The Kingdom of Shu was a weak state with a small population, situated on the frontier of the southwest. It was burdened with heavy military expenses. Coins used in Shu were of large units, among which important examples include the *Zhibai Wu-Zhu*, *Zhibai Xiaoqian* and *Shu Wu-Zhu*.

• 直百五铢（三国 蜀）
Zhibai Wu-Zhu, Kingdom of Shu-Han
(Three Kingdoms Period, 220-280)

兵，军费不足，直百五铢减重严重。于是铸造了形体小、重量轻的直百小钱。多为民间私铸，钱体小，大小轻重不一，钱文平坦，"直百"二字，横读，背面有模铸文字或符号。

蜀五铢：为铸造直百小钱同时所铸。形体较小，面背有郭，面文多不清晰，"五铢"二字较肥硕，多不明晰，背面模铸阴文或纹饰。

孙吴钱币

孙吴铸行的钱币仿新莽大泉五十所铸，有"大泉五百""大泉当千""大泉二千""大泉五千"等，均为有名无实的大钱。其中大泉五百和大泉当千较为常见，其余均罕见。

大泉五百：嘉禾五年（236年）

Zhibai Wu-Zhu: It was cast in 214, when Liu Bei, founder of the Kingdom of Shu, took Chengdu. The *Zhibai Wu-Zhu*, one of which equaled a hundred normal *Wu-Zhu* coins, are large, inscribed on the obverse with *Zhibai Wu-Zhu* and on the reverse with the place name 为 (*Wei*) in relief. They were the earliest square-holed round coins inscribed with a place name by far.

Zhibai Xiaoqian: The small, light coin was cast in response to sharp reduction of the weight of *Zhibai Wu-Zhu* due to military deficit in the warring years toward the end of the Shu regime. Those coins were mostly cast by private organizations, and are uneven in size and weight. The flat characters 直百 on the obverse are horizontally inscribed, and intaglio characters or symbols are inscribed on the reverse.

Wu-Zhu of Shu: It was cast the same time as *Zhibai Xiaoqian*. They are small, with outlines on the obverse and reverse, and mostly inscribed with vague characters. The characters 五铢 on the obverse are fat and usually vague, while intaglio characters or patterns are inscribed on the reverse.

Coins of Sun-Wu

Coins of Wu were cast after the *Daquan Wushi* coins of the New Wang Mang

孙权铸行的钱币，以一枚当五百枚五铢钱使用，面背皆有内外郭，大小轻重不一，面文"大泉五百"。

Period, and include *Daquan Wubai*, *Daquan Dangqian*, *Daquan Erqian* and *Daquan Wuqian*, all worthing less than their nominal value. *Daquan Wubai* and *Daquan Dangqian* are more commonly seen, and the others are rare.

Daquan Wubai: It was cast in 236 in Sun Quan's reign, and each equaled five hundred *Wu-Zhu* coins. They have raised inner and outer rims on the obverse and reverse. The size and weight are not standardized. *Daquan Dangbai* is inscribed on the obverse.

- 大泉五百（三国 吴）
  Daquan Wubai, Kingdom of Wu (Three Kingdoms Period, 220-280)

- 大泉五百钱树（三国 吴）
  Cluster of *Daquan Wubai*, Kingdom of Wu (Three Kingdoms Period, 220-280)

大泉当千：赤乌元年（238年）孙权铸行的钱币，以一枚当一千枚五铢钱使用，面背皆有内外郭，大小轻重不一，不断减重，面文"大泉当千"，顺时针旋读。这种有名无实的大钱，使百姓深恶痛绝，纷纷抵制，于赤乌九年（246年）停

• 大泉当千（三国 吴）
Daquan Dangqian, Kingdom of Wu (Three Kingdoms Period, 220-280)

铸。

两晋钱币

两晋时期一直未曾铸钱，是中国货币史上的低谷时期。西晋主要沿用汉魏五铢钱和各种古钱，兼用谷帛等实物。

十六国钱币

十六国时期，出现了不以重量命名的国号钱和年号钱。如年号钱

Daquan Dangqian: They were coins cast in 238 under the order of Sun Quan, and each equaled a thousand *Wu-Zhu* coins. They have raised inner and outer rims on the obverse and reverse. The size and weight are not standardized, while the weight was incessantly reduced through time. The characters *Daquan Dangqian* are inscribed in a clockwise circle on the obverse. Those nominal coins were hated and boycotted by the common people, and the casting was put an end to in 246.

Coins of the Western Jin Dynasty (265-317) and the Eastern Jin Dynasty (317-420)

The Western Jin Dynasty and the Eastern Jin Dynasty were the low ebb of Chinese coinage development when no coins were cast. In the Western Jin Dynasty, people mainly used *Wu-Zhu* of the Kingdom of Wei and other ancient coins, while bartering by grain and silk on the side.

Coins of the Period of the Sixteen Kingdoms (304-439)

Coins named after states and periods instead of weight emerged during the period of the Sixteen kingdoms. Coins like the *Hanxing* coin and *Daxia*

• 汉兴钱（十六国 成汉）

Hanxing Coin, Cheng-Han State (Period of the Sixteen Kingdoms, 304-439)

"汉兴钱"等，"大夏真兴"更是融国号、年号于一体。

汉兴钱：李寿割据四川建成汉政权称帝，咸康四年（338年）改国号称汉，改元汉兴，铸汉兴钱。钱体薄小，钱文隶书，有直读和横读两种，多直读，是中国最早的以帝王年号命名的钱币。

丰货钱：东晋元帝大兴二年（319年）后赵国石勒铸造，钱文吉语，篆书，苍劲古拙，铸工不精。

大夏真兴：夏世祖武烈帝真兴元年（419年）赫连勃勃铸行，穿孔较大，铸作较精。钱文隶书，"大夏"是国号，"真兴"是年号，是首枚同铸国号与年号的钱币。

凉造新泉：凉州刺史张轨在河

Zhenxing combine state names and period names together.

Hanxing Coins: Li Shou of the Cheng-Han State (304-338) took Sichuan, claimed the throne and changed the state name to Han in 338. He adopted the reign title of *Hanxing* and cast the *Hanxing* coins. Those coins are small and thin, with inscription in the clerical style, either vertical or, less frequently, horizontal. They were the earliest Chinese coins named after the reigning periods of emperors and kings.

Fenghuo Coins: They were cast under the order of Shi Le, ruler of the State of Later Zhao, in 319. The characters *Feng Huo*, meaning afuence, are inscribed roughly yet vigorously in the seal style. The craftsmanship is not refined.

Daxia Zhenxing: They were issued by Helian Bobo, formally Emperor Wulie of Xia in 419, the 1st year of the Zhenxing Period. Those coins are exquisitely cast, with a large hole and inscription in the clerical style. The characters inscribed, "大夏" (*Diaxia*) means the great State of Xia and "真兴" (*Zhenxing*) the reign title. They were the earliest coins inscribed with both a state name and a period name.

Liangzao Xinquan: They were cast

西建立前凉政权所铸行，形制轻薄，钱文瘦小，顺读。

南朝钱币

南朝时期，江南经济有了较大发展，货币的铸造及使用范围都较两晋时期有所增加，造成币制混乱的局面。私铸成风，使铸币不断减重，劣钱泛滥。

刘宋钱币

刘宋时期的铸币主要有"四铢钱""孝建四铢""永光""两铢钱""景和"等。

四铢钱：宋文帝元嘉七年（430年）仿汉五铢钱铸造，铜质较粗，面背皆有边郭，钱文横读，背面光素或有星纹，有的面部也有星纹。

- 两铢钱（南朝 宋）

Liang-zhu Coins (Song of the Southern Dynasties, 420-479)

when Zhang Gui, former provincial governor of Liangzhou (present northwest of Gansu) established the regime of Former Liang in Hexi (present-day parts of Gansu and Qinghai in the west of the Yellow River). They are light and thin, with tiny inscription, and are read in regular order.

Coins of the Southern Dynasties

In the Southern dynasties, economy in the south of the lower reaches of the Yangtze River gained remarkable development, and both the amount of coins cast and the area of circulation increased. As a result, the monetary system was disturbed and private coin casting was rampant, leading to repeated reduction in coin weight and an overflow of bad coins.

Coins of the Song of the Southern Dynasties (420-479)

Coins cast in the Song of the Southern Dynasties mainly include the *Sizhu, Xiaojian Sizhu, Yongguang, Liangzhu* and *Jinghe*.

Si-Zhu Coins: They were an imitation of *Wu-Zhu* of the Han Dynasty, cast in 430 with less refined alloy. They have raised edges on the obverse and reverse. The characters are inscribed

- 景和钱（南朝 宋）
Jinghe Coin (Song of the Southern Dynasties, 420-479)

孝建四铢：孝建元年（454年）铸造，钱体大小不等，面文"孝建"，背文"四铢"，字体纤秀飘逸，背有星纹。

永光、两铢、景和：废帝刘子业永光元年（465年）铸造，都是二铢小钱，钱小穿大。

萧齐钱币

萧齐立国，实行货币紧缩政策，仅铸过一次为数不多的钱币。齐武帝永明八年（490年），在四川严道铜山（今雅安荥经）西汉邓通铸钱旧址，曾铸过不少铜钱，因成本过高而止。这次铸钱的形制特征在史书上未有记载。

萧梁钱币

萧梁时期铸造的钱币主要有"天监五铢""公式女钱""五铢铁

horizontally, and the reverse is left blank or inscribed with stars. Some have stars inscribed on the obverse.

Xiaojian Sizhu: They were cast in 454. They are unequal in size. On the obverse is inscribed *Xiaojian* and on the reverse *Sizhu* in an elegant style. The reverse is also decorated with star patterns.

Yongguang, Liangzhu and *Jinghe*: They were all cast in 465 in the short-lived reign of Liu Ziye. They are all small coins worth two *Zhu*, with a big hole.

Coins of the Xiao-Qi Dynasty (479-502)

When Xiao-Qi was established by the Xiao family, a deflation policy was carried out and only one coin casting was organized, producing a small amount of coins. In 490, a large amount of coins were cast in Tongshan, Yandao in Sichuan (present Yingjing in Ya'an) where Deng Tong of the Western Han Dynasty had organized coin casting. But this activity had to be ended due to high cost. The characteristics of coins cast are not recorded in history.

Coins of the Xiao-Liang Dynasty (502-557)

Coins of the Xiao-Liang Dynasty are mainly the *Tianjian Wu-Zhu, Gongshi Nüqian, Wu-Zhu Tieqian, Erzhu Wu-Zhu* or *Sizhu Wu-Zhu*.

钱""二柱五铢""四柱五铢"等。

天监五铢：梁武帝于天监元年（502年）铸造，钱文"五铢"，铸造精整，面背皆有内外郭。

公式女钱：同天监五铢同年铸造，钱体轻小，铸作粗糙，边郭被磨去或凿去，无外郭。

五铢铁钱：梁武帝普通四年（523年）铸造的铁钱，有大吉五铢、大富五铢、大通五铢铁钱三品，大吉、大通、大富皆为吉祥吉语。五铢铁钱形制不一，中厚边薄，铸造粗劣，背有四出纹。这是中国钱币史上第一次大规模铸造铁钱，以铁钱代替铜钱。

Tianjian Wu-Zhu: They were cast in 502, the 1st year of the Tianjian Period under Emperor Wu of Liang. They are neatly cast, with the inscription 五铢 and inner and outer rims on the obverse and reverse.

Gongshi Nüqian: they were cast the same year as *Tianjian Wu-Zhu*. They are small and light rimless coins, crudely made with the scraped rims.

Wu-Zhu Tieqian: They were iron coins cast in 523 under Emperor Wu of Liang, inscribed with the auspicious words *Daji* (great fortune), *Dafu* (great wealth) or *Datong* (great success). Their craftsmanship is inferior, and sizes not standardized. Those coins are thick in the middle and thin at the rim, with the inscription in relief of four lines radiating from the four corners of the square hole on the reverse. This was the first in Chinese coinage history of large-scale iron coin casting aiming to replace bronze coins.

Erzhu Wu-Zhu: They were cast during the Chengsheng Period under

太清丰乐（南朝 梁）
铸造于梁武帝太清时期，钱文为吉祥语"太清丰乐"。
Taiqing Fengle (Liang Dynasty, 502-557)
Coins cast in the Taiqing Period (547-549) under Emperor Wu of Liang, inscribed with the auspicious characters *Taiqing Fengle* meaning prosperity and happiness in the Taiqing Period.

二柱五铢：梁元帝承圣年间铸造，钱文"五铢"，正面穿上穿下各铸一星，共两星，星又称柱，故称"二柱"。

四柱五铢：梁敬帝太平二年（557年）铸造，钱文"五铢"，面背穿孔上下各铸一星，共四星，故称"四柱"。

Emperor Yuan of Liang. They are inscribed with 五铢 on the obverse, with one star above and below the hole, hence the name *Erzhu*, meaning two stars.

Sizhu Wu-Zhu: They were cast in the 2nd year of Taiping Period (557) under Emperor Jing of Liang. They are inscribed with 五铢 on the obverse, with one star above and below the hole both on the obverse and reverse, hence the name *Sizhu*, meaning four stars.

铁钱

铁金属在中国发现得较早，早在先秦时期，铁就被大量用来铸造农具。然而，很久之后才出现用铁铸造的钱币。最早用铁铸造的钱币是西汉初期铸造的"铁半两"。三国时期也铸过少量铁钱，然仅通行于一时一地，到了南北朝的梁代，铁钱才作为主币大量铸造流通。五代十国的楚、闽、燕等朝代以铸造铁钱而著名。宋代，铁钱盛行。宋代以后，铁钱的铸造就大为减少。

南朝梁武帝铸造铁钱，始于普通四年（523年）。这是中国货币史上第一次用铁钱代替铜钱，以铁钱为法定本位货币。梁朝铸行铁钱一是因为铜材缺乏；二是佛寺门阀士族聚敛成风，数量惊人，铜钱不敷流通，才造成了铁钱的盛行。

Iron Coins

Iron was found in a relatively early time in China. As early as in the Qin Dynasty, iron was widely employed to make agricultural implements. However, iron coins didn't appear until very late, when iron *Ban-Liang* coins were cast in the early years of the Western Han Dynasty. A few iron coins were also cast during the Three Kingdoms Period, but they only circulated for a short while within limited boundaries. It was not until the Liang Dynasty that iron coins became the mainstream currency to be cast and used in mass. States like Chu, Min and Yan in the period of the Five dynasties and Ten states were famous for iron coin casting. The Song Dynasty witnessed the apex of iron coins, and after that, iron coin casting plunged.

Emperor Wu of Liang began to have iron coins cast in 523, initiating in the Chinese coinage history the first replacement of bronze coins with iron ones as the legal and standard currency. This decision was compelled on the one hand by a deficiency in copper, and on the other by the extraordinary hoarding of copper coins by temples and families of power and influence, which hampered the circulation of copper coins and urged the use of iron ones.

陈朝钱币

陈朝钱币轮郭深峻，铸造精美，以"天嘉五铢"和"太货六铢"最为精致。

天嘉五铢：天嘉三年（562年），陈文帝铸造。铸造精工，有内外郭，外郭较宽，钱文"五铢"，"五"字似两个对顶的等腰三角形，"铢"字的"金"旁小于"朱"部，钱背多光素，偶有纹饰。

太货六铢：太建十一年（579年），陈宣帝陈顼铸造。铸作精美绝伦，居南朝钱币之冠，面背肉好，周郭整齐。面文字体端庄凝重、古朴飘逸。"太货"即大化、大钱的意思，起初一枚太货六铢比价10枚五铢钱，后来与五铢钱等值。如此贬值，民间怨声载道，纷传钱文"六"字犹人双手叉腰哭天

Coins of the Chen Dynasty (557-589)

Coins of the Chen Dynasty were exquisitely cast, with highly raised rims, among which the most refined being the *Tianjia Wu-Zhu* and *Taihuo Liuzhu* coins.

Tianjia Wu-Zhu: They were cast under the order of Emperor Wen of Chen in the 3rd year of the Tianjia Period (562). Exquisitely cast, those coins have both the inner and the outer rims, with the latter wider than the former. 五铢 are inscribed, with " 五 " (*Wu*) looking like a sandglass and " 铢 " (*Zhu*) larger at the right half. The reverse is usually left blank, though occasionally decorated with patterns.

Taihuo Liuzhu: They were issued by Emperor Xuan of Chen in 579. They are of extraordinarily refined craftsmanship, with neat rims, ranking the first among all coins of the Southern dynasties. The characters, *Taihuo Liuzhu*, *Taihuo*

• 太货六铢拓本（南朝 陈）
Rubbings of *Taihuo Liuzhu* (Chen Dynasty, 557-589)

子状，预示不祥。陈亡后，太货六铢成为有名的丧钱。

北朝钱币

北朝各政权所铸钱币大体上比南朝好，形制均为方孔圆钱，有内外郭，外郭较宽，钱文均记值。

北魏钱币

北魏直到孝文帝迁都后才铸造钱币，所铸钱币有"太和五铢""永平五铢"和"永安五铢"三种。

太和五铢：北魏孝文帝太和十九年（495年）铸造，钱体大小不一。面文"太和五铢"。

永平五铢：北魏宣武帝永平三年（510年）铸造，制作粗劣，版式复杂，大小轻重不一。面文"五铢"，模糊难辨。

meaning large coin, are inscribed in a plain but elegant style. At first the coin was equivalent to ten *Wu-Zhu*. Later the value was reduced to one, which aroused great discontent among the common people, who insisted that the character " 六 " (*Liu*, six) on the coin resembled ominously a man crying for Emperor, his arms akimbo. Those coins thus became notorious money of mourning after the Chen Dynasty collapsed.

Coins of the Northern Dynasties

Coins issued by regimes in the Northern dynasties are generally superior to those from the Southern dynasties. They are all square-holed round coins, with inner and outer rims, the latter wider than the former, and an inscription of value.

Coins of the Northern Wei Dynasty (386-534)

No coins were issued in the Northern Wei Dynasty until Emperor Xiaowen moved the capital from Pingcheng (in present Datong, Shanxi) to Luoyang. Three types of coins were cast after then, namely the *Taihe Wu-Zhu, Yongping Wu-Zhu* and *Yong'an Wu-Zhu*.

Taihe Wu-Zhu: They were issued in the 19th year of Taihe Period (495) by

太和五铢（北朝 北魏）
Taihe Wu-Zhu (Northern Wei Dynasty, 386-534)

永安五铢：北魏孝庄帝永安二年（529年）铸造，铸作工整，大小轻重不一。面文"永安五铢"，直读。

东魏、西魏钱币

东魏和西魏沿用永安五铢钱。东魏孝静帝武定初年（543年）曾改铸，钱文仍为"永安五铢"。西魏大统六年（540年），文帝铸五铢钱，大统十二年（546年）又铸"大统五铢"。西魏五铢钱与永安五铢钱形制相近，制作粗糙。

Emperor Xiaowen. They are uneven in size, and have the inscription of *Taihe Wu-Zhu*.

Yongping Wu-Zhu: They were cast under the order of Emperor Xuanwu in the 3rd year of Yongping Period (510). They are crudely made, with many variations in shape size and weight. The inscription *Wu Zhu* is vague to the degree of illegible.

Yong'an Wu-Zhu: They were issued by Emperor Xiaozhuang in the 2nd year of Yong'an Period (529). They are neatly cast, with no standard in size or weight. The inscription *Yong'an Wu-Zhu* is read vertically.

Coins of the Eastern Wei Dynasty (534-550) and the Western Wei Dynasty (535-556)

Yong'an Wu-Zhu was used in the Eastern Wei Dynasty and the Western Wei Dynasty. In 543, Emperor Xiaojing of the Eastern Wei Dynasty reformed the shape of this coin, but the inscription remained the same. In 540, Emperor Wen of the Western Wei Dynasty had *Wu-Zhu* cast, and then in 546 issued the *Datong*

五铢钱（北朝 西魏）
Wu-Zhu Coin (Western Wei Dynasty, 535-556)

北齐钱币

北齐之初仍沿用永安五铢。天保四年（553年），文宣帝改铸"常平五铢"，铸作精美，钱面平整，面文"常平五铢"，笔画流畅。后来，常平五铢成为一种不足值的大钱，私铸渐多，版别较多，甚至出现铜中掺铁铸钱的现象。

- 常平五铢（北朝 北齐）
Changping Wu-Zhu (Northern Qi Dynasty, 550-577)

北周钱币

布泉、五行大布、永通万国俗称"北周三钱"，皆为虚值大钱，铸造精美，被誉为六朝钱币之冠。钱文笔法华美，篆法绝工，具有很高的艺术价值。然而，一个比一个减重，贬值厉害。

布泉：铸于武帝保定元年（561年），制作精整，面背肉好皆有周

Wu-Zhu coins. *Wu-Zhu* of the Western Wei Dynasty are similar to those of the Yong'an Period, both are roughly made.

Coins of the Northern Qi Dynasty (550-577)

Yong'an Wu-Zhu was still in use in the early Northern Qi Dynasty. In 553, Emperor Wenxuan issued the *Changping Wu-Zhu*, which are exquisitely cast and carved by the inscriptions of *Changping Wu-Zhu*, with neat surfaces and smooth strokes of characters. Later, *Changping Wu-Zhu* was reduced to large coins of little value, and as private coin casting increased, the form of the coins began to vary, and even the alloy was deteriorated by adulteration with iron.

Coins of the Northern Zhou Dynasty (557-581)

Coins inscribed with *Buquan, Wuxing Dabu* or *Yongtong Wanguo* are known as the three major coins of the Northern Zhou Dynasty. They are large coins with high nominal values, so exquisitely cast that they were deemed the best of coins of this period of time. The inscription is neat and graceful, of high artistic value. However, the weights of those coins were continually reduced and they depreciated greatly.

Buquan: They were cast in 561 under the order of Emperor Wu of the

郭，隆起整齐，一枚当五铢五枚使用。面文"布泉"，横读，玉箸篆，笔画肥满圆润，温厚。私铸者钱体轻小，多呈青白色。

北周布泉和新莽布泉不同。一是钱文书体不同：北周布泉是玉箸篆，新莽布泉是悬针篆；二是泉字的书写有别：北周布泉的"泉"字，中竖不断，上下贯通；新莽布泉的"泉"字中竖上下断开。

五行大布：铸于建德三年（574年），制作精细，面背肉好皆有周郭，以一枚当布泉十枚使用。钱形体大小、轻重不一。面文"五行大布"，直读，玉箸篆，俊丽秀美。五行大布取阴阳五行学说的相生相克、循环不息之理，寓流通之意，然而后来由于私铸甚多，被禁止出入四关。

永通万国：铸于静帝宇文阐大象元年（579年），制作甚精，肉好面背皆有周郭，有合背者，钱体厚重，大小轻重不一，一枚当五行大布十枚使用。铜色青白，钱文"永通万国"，直读，铁线篆，笔画圆活纤细，细硬如铁。"永通万国"有长久流通之意。永通万国铅钱，被认为是铅钱的始祖。

Northern Zhou Dynasty. They are neatly cast, with evenly raised inner and outer rims on the obverse and the reverse. One *Buquan* was equivalent to five *Wu-Zhu* coins. The inscription *Buquan* is written in the *Yuzhu* (jade chopsticks) seal script with full and soft strokes, and is read horizontally. Privately cast coins are light and small, usually of a pale green color.

The *Buquan* of the Northern Zhou Dynasty is different from the one of the Xinmang Period. Firstly, the font of the inscription is different: the Northern Zhou's is written in *Yuzhu Zhuan*, while the Xinmang Period's is written in *Xuanzhen Zhuan*. Secondly, the character *Quan* is written differently: the Northern Zhou's *Quan* is with its middle vertical line written thoroughly from top to bottom, while the Xinmang Period's *Quan* is with its middle vertical line disconnected.

Wuxing Dabu: They were cast in 574. They are refined, with inner and outer rims on the obverse and reverse. One such coin was intended to be worth ten *Buquan* coins. The size and weight vary. The inscription *Wuxing Dabu* are gracefully inscribed in the *Yuzhu Zhuan* (jade chopsticks seal style) and read vertically. This coin bears the meaning of everlasting circulation, as indicated by the Five Elements which depend on and give support to each other in unending cycles. However, illegal coining became so rampant that the authorities eventually banned the use of this coin.

Yongtong Wanguo: The coins were cast in 579 by Emperor Jing. They are made with highly refined craftsmanship, with inner and outer rims on the obverse and the reverse. It has cover and back. Those coins are thick and heavy, with no standard size or weight. One such coin was meant to be equivalent to ten *Wuxing Dabu* coins. They have a pale green color. The characters *Yongtong Wanguo* are in the iron wire seal style, with thin, flexible yet forceful strokes, and are read vertically. This inscription bears the wish to circulate for a long time. Lead coins inscribed with *Yongtong Wanguo* are deemed the ancestor of later lead coins.

- 北周三钱（北朝 北周）
  从上到下依次为布泉、五行大布和永通万国。
  Three Coins of the Northern Zhou Dynasty (Northern Zhou Dynasty, 557-581)
  From the top to the bottom are the *Buquan*, *Wuxing Dabu* and *Yongtong Wanguo*.

铅钱

中国是世界上最早以铅铸钱的国家，但是关于铅钱铸于何时，众说纷纭。有的说是起源于五代后梁，有的说是北朝北周，也有说是周代和战国，没有一个标准的说法。

按目前出土实物来看，铅铸造始于战国时期的燕国。大量出现铅钱是在五代时期，五代以后多不铸造铅钱。大部分铅钱只是流通于一时一地。

Lead Coins

China is the first country in the world to cast lead coins. However, there is no agreement as regard when lead coins were first cast: some believe that it originated in the Later Liang Dynasty, while others hold that it was in the Northern Zhou Dynasty, and still others attribute it to the Zhou Dynasty or the Warring States Period.

Judged from the relics in hand, the casting of lead coins originated in the State Yan during the Warring States Period. A hoard of lead coins appeared in the Five dynasties, and few lead coins have been cast since. Most lead coins only circulated for a short time in a small area.

- 永隆通宝铅钱（十国）
  Lead Coin of *Yonglong Tongbao* (Five Dynasties and Ten States, 907-960)

> 隋唐钱币

隋五铢

隋五铢有两种：一种是隋文帝开皇六年至仁寿四年铸行"开皇五铢"；另一种是隋炀帝大业年间铸行的"五铢白钱"。

开皇五铢

开皇五铢又称"置样五铢"，铸造精美，肉好，有周郭，边郭较阔，大小轻重不一。面文"五铢"，横读，铢字"金"旁右敛，"五"字左侧靠近方孔处有一竖画，曲笔相交，转过来看像个"凶"字，时人认为有不祥之兆。

五铢白钱

五铢白钱的铸币材料中加重了锡和铅的含量，因而钱色发白，故称"白钱"。铸作精整，形制与开

> Currencies of the Sui Dynasty (581-618) and Tang Dynasty (618-907)

Wu-Zhu of the Sui Dynasty

Wu-Zhu of the Sui Dynasty includes two types, the *Kaihuang Wu-Zhu* issued from 581 to 604 by Emperor Wen of Sui, and the *Wu-Zhu Baiqian* issued by Emperor Yang of Sui from 605 to 618.

Kaihuang Wu-Zhu

Kaihuang Wu-Zhu, also called *Zhiyang Wu-Zhu*, is exquisitely cast with inner and outer rims, the latter wider than the former. They are uneven in size and weight. The characters *Wu Zhu*, read horizontally, are inscribed in such a way that the left part of " 铢 " (*Zhu*) leaning towards right, and " 五 " (*Wu*), shaped like a sandglass, has a vertical line on its left, making it seem like the character "凶" (*Xiong*), which means bad omen, when turned anti-clockwise

- 开皇五铢拓本
  Rubbing of a *Kaihuang Wu-Zhu*

- 五铢白钱（隋）
  Wu-Zhu Baiqian (Sui Dynasty, 581-618)

皇五铢相同，面文"五铢"，横读，笔画细长，"五"字交笔处弧曲，背有月纹。

五铢白钱的制作，上承魏制，接近北魏的"永安五铢"；下启唐初白钱的铸造，唐开元钱，色青白，轮郭阔厚，与五铢白钱相似。

唐代钱币

唐初仍沿用隋代旧钱，唐高祖武德四年（621年）下令废五铢，铸"开元通宝"，此后钱币开始以记

90 degrees. For this reason, those coins were considered ominous by contemporary people.

Wu-Zhu Baiqian

The whitish colour of those coins is the result of the addition of lead and tin to the alloy, which gives them the name *Baiqian*, white coins. They are neatly cast, similar to *Kaihuang Wu-Zhu* in form. The inscription *Wu Zhu*, read horizontally, has long, slender strokes. The character "五" (*Wu*) is more like a sandglass for the intersecting strokes are curved. The reverse is inscribed with moon pattern.

The casting of *Wu-Zhu Baiqian* followed the tradition of the Northern Wei Dynasty, producing coins resembling the *Yong'an Wu-Zhu*, and anticipated the coining of the *Baiqian* of the early Tang Dynasty. The inaugural coins of Tang resemble *Wu-Zhu Baiqian* in being whitish, with wide outer rim.

Coins of the Tang Dynasty

Coins from the Sui Dynasty were used in the early Tang Dynasty. In 621, Emperor Gaozu of the Tang Dynasty abolished *Wu-Zhu* and issued the coins inscribed with *Kaiyuan Tongbao*. Since then, coin inscriptions are mainly carved with reign

年为主。

开元通宝

开元通宝，又称"武德开元"，制作精美，铜质纯净，面背肉好，轮郭平整，钱背平素无纹，稍后出现星纹、月纹及其他纹饰。钱文"开元通宝"为唐代书法家欧阳询所书隶书，深竣清晰、端庄大气。"开元"有开辟新纪元的意思，不是指代年号。钱背常有一道指甲痕，相传是进呈蜡样时，文德皇后指甲所留。开元通宝的形制因铸年长久，故有多种样式。

开元通宝除有青铜质地外，唐初还铸造有金、银、铅、铁、陶质地和鎏金的开元通宝。这些质地的开元通宝多作为宫钱和冥币，专门用于赏赐和殉葬，不参与流通。金、银质地的

- 开元通宝（唐）
Kaiyuan Tongbao (Tang Dynasty, 618-907)

titles.

Kaiyuan Tongbao

Kaiyuan Tongbao is also called Wude Kaiyuan. They are exquisitely cast with pure copper, with neat inner and outer rims on the obverse and reverse. The reverse of early-cast coins is left blank, and that of later ones is inscribed with patterns like stars, the moon, etc. The inscription Kaiyuan Tongbao is written by famous calligrapher Ouyang Xun in the clerical style. The characters look elegant and majestic, with clear and firm strokes. Kaiyuan is not a period name but means to usher in a new era. Usually on the reverse there is a mark impressed by a finger nail, which is reported to have been made by Empress Wende on the wax sample presented to Emperor. As the Kaiyuan Tongbao was issued for many years, there are variations in the form.

Besides the bronze Kaiyuan Tongbao, there were also gold, silver, lead, iron, earthen and gilded Kaiyuan Tongbao used in the early Tang Dynasty, but those coins were mainly used as rewards in the palace or as funeral accompaniments instead of circulating in the market. Gold and silver Kaiyuan Tongbao must have been used as rewards, while earthen ones as funeral

开元通宝应作为赏赐钱,陶质的则为冥币。陕西还发现了玳瑁雕刻的开元通宝,应为供佛特制。

开元通宝的出现,是中国古代钱币史上的一次重大飞跃,确立了一两十钱制的衡法,开启了中国铸币以通宝为名称的先河。此后的方孔圆钱,多以"通宝""元宝""重宝"和"泉宝"相称,前面还冠以年号。

money. *Kaiyuan Tongbao* carved out of hawksbill shells have been found in Shaanxi, which are believed to have been used as offer to Buddha.

The appearance of *Kaiyuan Tongbao* marked a great leap in Chinese coinage history, as it completed the measurement units in which one *Liang* equaled ten coins and initiated the nomenclature of coins by *Tongbao*. Since then, square-hole round coins have been named *Tongbao*, *Yuanbao*, *Zhongbao* or *Quanbao*, accompanied with a period name.

元宝

"元宝"是对金银货币的通称,它来源于对"开元通宝"的旋读——"开通元宝"。

唐肃宗乾元二年(759年),史思明在洛阳铸的"得壹元宝",是最早以元宝命名货币者。得壹元宝,宽缘,楷书隶意,钱文旋读。同年,史思明改铸"顺天元宝"大钱,形制与得壹元宝相同。

后来,唐代宗铸有"大历元宝",后晋铸有"天福元宝",北宋的"淳化元宝""圣宗元宝",南宋的"大宋元宝",元初的"中统元宝"以及清末的"光绪元宝"铜元,均以"元宝"相称。

• 得壹元宝(唐)
Deyi Yuanbao (Tang Dynasty, 618-907)

Yuanbao

Yuanbao is the name for all gold and silver currencies, which was invented when the inscription *Kaiyuan Tongbao* is read as *Kaitong Yuanbao* in revolving order.

The first coin to be named *Yuanbao* was *Deyi Yuanbao*, cast under the order of Shi Siming in Luoyang, in 759, under Emperor Suzong of Tang. This type of coin has a broad rim, with the inscription written in the *Kaishu*, or the regular script, reminiscent of the clerical style, and arranged in a clockwise circle. Shi Siming issued another currency the same year, the *Shuntian Yuanbao*, which is similar to the *Deyi Yuanbao*.

Yuanbao issued afterward included the *Dali Yuanbao* of the Tang Dynasty, *Tianfu Yuanbao* of the Later Jin Dynasty, *Chunhua Yuanbao* and *Shengzong Yuanbao* of the Northern Song Dynasty, *Dasong Yuanbao* of the Southern Song Dynasty, *Zhongtong Yuanbao* of the early Yuan Dynasty and *Guangxu Yuanbao* of the late Qing Dynasty.

● 顺天元宝鎏金钱（唐）
**Gilded *Shuntian Yuanbao*
(Tang Dynasty, 618-907)**

● 元宝（图片提供：图虫创意）
元宝也特指船形的金铤、银铤，其中间部分没有凸出的形状，后来基于它的形状有点像棺材，为人们所忌讳，所以将中间的部分做成凸出的形状，成为我们如今所见的元宝，具有招财进宝的吉祥寓意。

Yuanbao

The name *Yuanbao* can also refer to a kind of gold or silver ingot originally shaped like a boat with a flat cabin and reformed later, due to this shape resembled ominously the coffin, to the commonly seen sycee with a dome in the middle, with the propitious message of bringing in wealth.

唐朝的其他铜钱

除了开元通宝以外，唐朝还铸有乾封、乾元、建中、会昌、咸通等铜钱。

乾封元年（666年），唐高宗铸"乾封泉宝"；乾元元年（758年），唐肃宗铸"乾元重宝"，与开元通宝并用，以一当十；乾元二年（759年）改铸重轮乾元重宝，即钱背外郭呈双重状，一枚重轮钱当五十个开元钱流通使用，此钱在唐后期贬值严重，只当一文开元钱；建中年间，唐德宗铸有"建中通宝"小平钱，钱体轻薄，制作粗劣；会昌五年（845年），唐武宗毁佛像、法器铸"会昌开元"钱，钱体轻小，背铸"昌"字等20多个地名；唐懿宗咸通十一年（870年），铸过"咸通玄宝"。

Other Copper Coins of the Tang Dynasty

Besides *Kaiyuan Tongbao*, there were other copper coins including *Qianfeng, Qianyuan, Jianzhong, Huichang* and *Xiantong* circulating in the Tang Dynasty.

In 666, the 1st year of the the Qianfeng Period, Emperor Gaozong of Tang issued the *Qianfeng Quanbao*. In 758, the 1st year of the Qianyuan Period, Emperor Suzong issued the *Qianyuan Zhongbao*, which was to be used alongside *Kaiyuan Tongbao* and each of which was worth ten *Kaiyuan Tongbao* coins. The next year (759), a new type of coin, the *Chonglun Qianyuan*

• 乾封泉宝（唐）、乾封泉宝鎏金钱（唐）

乾封泉宝是唐代第一枚年号钱，铸造精美，钱文楷书，存世不多。

Qianfeng Quanbao (Tang Dynasty, 618-907), Gilded *Qianfeng Quanbao* (Tang Dynasty, 618-907)

Qianfeng Quanbao was the first coin of the Tang Dynasty inscribed with reign title. They are exquisitely cast, with inscription in the regular style. A few of them have been found.

• 乾元重宝母钱正面

Front of the Mother Coin of *Qianyuan Zhongbao* (Tang Dynasty, 618-907)

• 乾元重宝母钱背面（唐）

Back of the Mother Coin of *Qianyuan Zhongbao* (Tang Dynasty, 618-907)

Zhongbao, i.e. the *Qianyuan Zhongbao* with double outer rims, was issued, each to be equivalent to fifty *Kaiyuan Tongbao* coins. In the late Tang Dynasty, this coin was depreciated so much that one was only worth one *Kaiyuan Tongbao* coin. During the Jianzhong Period (780-783), Emperor Dezong issued the *Jianzhong Tongbao*, a light and thin small coin crudely cast. In 845, the 5th year of the Huichang Period, Emperor Wuzong destroyed the Buddha statues and instruments to use the copper to cast the *Huichang Kaiyuan* coins, which are light and small, inscribed on the reverse with the place name " 昌 " (*Chang*) or other more than twenty place names. In 870, the 11th year of the Xiantong Period, Emperor Yizong issued the *Xiantong Xuanbao*.

- 乾元重宝（唐）
乾元重宝是最早的重宝钱，版别复杂，钱文隶书，形制不一。
Qianyuan Zhongbao (Tang Dynasty, 618-907)
Qianyuan Zhongbao was the first *Zhongbao* coin, with varied versions designs and inscription in the clerical style.

- 高昌吉利（唐）
高昌吉利为西部高昌国（今新疆）于贞观年间所铸，制作精美，钱体厚重，钱文隶书。
Gaochang Jili (Tang Dynasty, 618-907)
Gaochang Jili was cast by the Kingdom Gaochang in present Xinjiang in the Zhenguan Period. They are exquisite, thick and heavy, with inscription in the clerical style.

金银铸币

唐代的金银铸币主要用作支付和储藏，也当做赏赐、官中玩赏的官钱使用。其可分为铤状、饼状和方孔圆形三种形制。

唐代的铤状金银铸币是最早铸造的金银铤。铸成铤状的黄金，称为"金铤"。铸成铤状的白银，称为"银铤"。铤是四边平齐的长条形，与笏相像，也称作笏。笏是手

Gold and Silver Money

Gold and silver money in the Tang Dynasty was mainly used for payment and conservation, or as reward or toy money in the palace, including the *Ding* (gold or silver block), gold or silver plate and the square-holed round coin.

Ding of the Tang Dynasty was cast the earliest. There are gold *Ding* made of gold and silver *Ding* made of silver, which are rectangular blocks resembling *Hu*, tablet held by someone having authority. Therefore *Ding* is also called

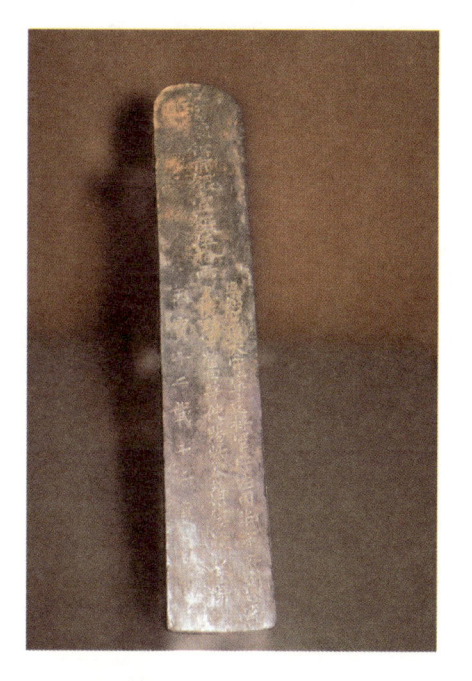

- 杨国忠进银铤（唐）
 Silver *Ding* of Yang GuoZhong (Tang Dynasty, 618-907)

- 岭南道税商银铤（唐）
 Taxation Silver *Ding* of Lingnan (Tang Dynasty, 618-907)

- 怀集庸调银饼（唐）
Yongdiao (Tax) Silver Plate of Huaiji
(Tang Dynasty, 618-907)

- 浒安庸调银饼（唐）
Yongdiao (Tax) Silver Plate of Jian'an
(Tang Dynasty, 618-907)

板，称笏者，多是五十两重的大银铤；金铤多为小形，不称笏。银铤轻重、大小不一。有的中间厚，周围薄，有的钱文中有年月、重量、人名等内容。

Hu. The *Ding* is mostly large silver block weighing fifty *Liang*. Gold *Ding* is usually small and can not be called as *Hu*. Silver *Ding* has no standard of the weight and size. Some are thick in the middle and thin around the edge, while some are inscribed with year, month, weight, people's names, etc.

There are gold and silver plates, not strictly round, with the reverse slightly caved in. Gold plates were made by

- 开元通宝银钱（唐）
Silver *Kaiyuan Tongbao* (Tang Dynasty, 618-907)

饼状的金银有金饼、银饼，形状略呈圆形，背面略低凹。金饼是把金熔化倾倒在坛子里形成的，故又称为"坛子金"。

唐代还铸有方孔圆形金银钱，如开元通宝金钱和银钱。

melting gold and molding in a jar, and therefore the gold plate is also known as the "jar gold".

In the Tang Dynasty, gold and silver square-holed round coins were issued, such as the gold and silver *Kaiyuan Tongbao* coins.

飞钱

唐宪宗年间，经济发达，商人在外做买卖时不方便随身携带大量钱币，于是他们在京城把货物卖出去以后，就可把钱交到本道（古代道用来代称地方一级行政单位，相当于现代的省）的进奏院（地方行政在长安设的代表办事处），领取一张收据，上面写明姓名、金额和日期，然后当面把这张收据分为两半，其中半张商人随身带着，另半张则寄回本道。等回本道后，商人再凭着半张收据，到当地指定部门兑换现钱。若两张半券能无误地合起来，就可以领回现钱。这种看起来像是在收据上飞来飞去的钱就被称为"飞钱"，也叫"便换"。

飞钱虽已接近纸币的性质，但由于不介入流通，不行使货币的职能，不是真正意义上的纸币，只是一种汇兑业务形式。

Flying Money

The economy was developed in the reign of Emperor Xianzong of Tang. It was not convenient for traveling merchants to carry along large sums of money, and so after they had sold his goods in the capital, he could deposit the money at the offices set in the capital by his local provincial administration, in exchange for a receipt with his name, the sum of money and date on it. This receipt was divided into two halves, one kept by the merchant, and the other sent back to the administration of his province. When he returned, he could exchange cash at an appointed office with his half receipt if the two halves matched. In this way, money seemed to be flying across regions on a piece of receipt, hence the name flying money. It was also called *Bianhuan*, convenient exchange.

The flying money was very close to paper currency, but since no circulation was involved and no function of currency performed, the flying money was still no strict paper currency but merely a means of agiotage.

> 五代十国钱币

五代钱币

　　五代时期朝代更替频繁，各政权均铸有钱币，但种类和数量较少。后梁铸有大钱"开平元宝"和"开平通宝"；后唐仿开元钱形制，铸有"天成元宝"；后晋铸行"天福元宝"；后汉铸造"汉元通宝"；后周铸有"周元通宝"。

- 天成元宝（五代 后唐）
Tiancheng Yuanbao (Later Tang Dynasty, 923-936)

> Currencies of the Five Dynasties and Ten States (907-960)

Coins of the Five Dynasties (907–960)

Although the dynasties during the Five dynasties altered frequently and all had their own coins issued, only a few types and amounts of coins were cast. The Later Liang Dynasty (907-923) issued coins with large face value *Kaiping Yuanbao* and *Kaiping Tongbao*; the Later Tang Dynasty (923-936) issued *Tiancheng Yuanbao* which was in imitation of the design of *Kaiyuan* currency; the Later Jin Dynasty (936-947) issued *Tianfu Yuanbao*; the Later Han Dynasty (947-950) issued *Hanyuan Tongbao*; and the Later Zhou Dynasty (951-960) issued *Zhouyuan Tongbao*.

　　Zhouyuan Tongbao, cast from the melted copper Buddha statues and based on the pattern of *Kaiyuan Tongbao* in

"周元通宝"居五代钱币之冠，它是后周世宗柴荣在显德二年（955年）熔铸铜佛像，仿开元通宝铸成。钱体精美，钱文隶意，旋读，背多铸有星纹和月纹。由于周元通宝取材于佛像，与佛结缘，所以民间传说此钱有神奇的功能，能辟邪，能治病。民间多仿周元通宝铸造花钱，用于佩带、赠送或玩赏。

这一时期，一些较小的政权也铸有钱币，如盘踞幽州的燕国刘仁恭、刘守光父子铸有"永安一十""永安一百""永安一千""应圣元宝""乾圣元宝"等大量铁钱及少量铜钱。

the 2nd year of the Xiande Period (955) with the order of Chai Rong, Emperor Shizong of the Later Zhou, was the best-known coin among those in the Five dynasties. This type of coin is exquisitely manufactured, with characters in the clerical style read circularly, and the designs of stars and moons on the reverse. It was believed *Zhouyuan Tongbao* exorcized the evils and cured diseases as it was made from the statue of Buddha. In the hope of good luck, folks often counterfeited *Zhouyuan Tongbao* as ornaments, gifts or for entertainment.

Smaller regimes in this period also cast their own coins. Liu Rengong and Liu Shouguang, the father and son who

• 永安一百铜钱和铁钱（五代十国 燕）
Copper Coin and Iron Coin of *Yong'an Yibai*, State Yan (Five Dynasties and Ten States, 907-960)

• 永安一千铜钱和铁钱（五代十国 燕）
Copper Coin and Iron Coin of *Yong'an Yiqian*, State Yan (Five Dynasties and Ten States, 907-960)

十国钱币

十国中唯有楚、闽、南汉、前蜀、后蜀、南唐六个割据政权铸造过钱币，各国铸钱多粗制滥造，铅铁为材，种类繁杂。楚国铸有"天策府宝"铜、铁、鎏金钱，"乾封泉宝"铜、铁、铅钱，"乾元重宝"铜钱；闽国铸有"开元通宝"铜、铁、铅钱，"永隆通宝"铁、铅钱，"天德通宝"和"天德重宝"铜、铁钱；南汉铸有"乾亨重宝"铜、铅钱，"乾亨通宝"铜钱；前蜀铸有"永平元宝""通正元宝""天汉元宝""光天元宝""乾德元宝"和"咸康元宝"六种年号钱；后蜀铸有"广政通宝"与"大蜀通宝"铜、铁、铅

occupied Youzhou (the present Beijing) and established the State Yan (911-913), issued iron coins in large amount and a few copper coins such as *Yong'an Yishi*, *Yong'an Yiba*, *Yong'an Yiqian*, *Yingsheng Yuanbao* and *Qiansheng Yuanbao*.

Coins of the Ten States (907–979)

Only the Chu State (907-951), the Min State (909-945), the Southern Han State (917-971), the Former Shu State (903-925), the Later Shu State (933-965), and the Southern Tang State (937-975) among the ten states issued their own coins. Made from iron or lead, these coins were roughly manufactured and their types were too varied. Chu cast *Tiance Fubao* of copper, iron, and gilt, *Qianfeng Quanbao* of copper, iron, and

- 天策府宝鎏金钱（十国 楚）
  Gilted Coin of *Tiance Fubao*, State Chu (Ten States, 907-979)

- 永隆通宝铅钱（十国 闽）
  Lead Coin of *Yonglong Tongbao*, State Min (Ten States, 907-979)

钱；南唐铸行的钱币有"大齐通宝""保大元宝""永通泉货""开元通宝""唐国通宝"和"大唐通宝"等。

lead, and *Qianyuan Zhongbao* of copper. Min cast *Kaiyuan Tongbao* of copper, iron, and lead, *Yonglong Tongbao* of iron and lead, *Tiande Tongbao* and *Tiande Zhongbao* of copper and iron. The Southern Han cast *Qianheng Zhongbao* of copper and lead, and *Qianheng Tongbao* of copper. The Former Shu cast six types of period name coins *Yongping Yuanbao, Tongzheng Yuanbao, Tianhan Yuanbao, Guangtian Yuanbao, Qiande Yuanbao,* and *Xiankang Yuanbao*. The Later Shu cast *Guangzheng Tongbao* and *Dashu Tongbao* of copper, iron, and lead. The Southern Tang cast *Daqi Tongbao, Baoda Yuanbao, Yongtong Quanhuo, Kaiyuan Tongbao, Tangguo Tongbao, Datang Tongbao*, etc.

- 天德重宝（十国 闽）
  Tiande Zhongbao, State Min (Ten States, 907-979)

- 乾德元宝（十国 前蜀）
  Qiande Yuanbao, State Former Shu (Ten States, 907-979)

- 保大元宝铁钱（十国 南唐）
  Iron Coin of *Baoda Yuanbao*, State Southern Tang (Ten States, 907-979)

- 唐国通宝（十国 南唐）
  Tangguo Tongbao, State Southern Tang (Ten States, 907-979)

> 宋代钱币

> Currencies of the Song Dynasty (960-1279)

对钱

"对钱",又称"对文钱""对书钱""和合钱",指材质、形制、币值、钱文内容完全相同,而钱文书体不同的两枚钱。

对钱始铸于南唐,盛行于北宋。南唐中主李璟铸的"开元通宝"铜钱,是对钱之始。北宋先后铸行了"天圣元宝""明道元宝""皇宋通宝""至和元宝""治平元宝"等二十五种对钱,书体有篆、楷、行三种,以篆体为主。

南宋也铸有对钱,主要有"绍兴元宝""乾道元宝"对钱;伪齐政权刘豫也曾铸"阜昌通宝""阜昌元宝"对钱。

Pair Money

"Pair money", also called "pair character money", "pair inscription money", "pair combining money", which indicates two coins with completely same texture, shape and form, value and inscription, but different inscription calligraphy.

Pair money was firstly cast in the Southern Tang during the Ten States Period (902-979) and prevailed in the Northern Song Dynasty (960-1127). It started from the *Kaiyuan*

• 乾道元宝对钱(南宋)
Pair Money of *Qiandao Yuanbao* (Southern Song Dynasty, 1127-1279)

Tongbao copper coin founded by the king of Southern Tang, Li Jing. The Northern Song Dynasty successively cast *Tiansheng Yuanbao, Mingdao Yuanbao, Huangsong Tongbao, Zhihe Yuanbao, Zhiping Yuanbao*, etc., totally 25 kinds of pair money, with three calligraphy fonts, *Zhuan, Kai, Xing*, mainly with the font *Zhuan*.

The Southern Song Dynasty (1127-1279) also cast pair money, mainly *Shaoxing Yuanbao, Qiandao Yuanbao*; the king of the puppet Qi authority, Liu Yu also cast pair money like *Fuchang Tongbao, Fuchang Yuanbao*.

北宋铜铁钱

北宋钱币在数量和质量上都远超前代，钱币多以年号为钱文，9个皇帝共改了35次年号，铸有27种年号钱和3种非年号钱。

北宋钱币以铜钱为主，也有铁钱流通，有的地方铜钱和铁钱同时流通。北宋铜铁钱币铸造精良，钱名多是通宝、元宝，钱文书法优美，多为帝王、名家所书，具有很高的艺术价值。其中，以宋徽宗时期所铸钱最为精美，居宋钱之冠。

宋太宗时，铸有"宋元通宝""太平通宝""淳化元宝"和"至道元宝"。宋元通宝是仿周元通宝所铸的小平铜、铁钱，是北宋的第一种铸币。太平通宝则是北宋第一种

Copper Coins and Iron Coins in the Northern Song Dynasty (960-1127)

The quantity and quality of coins in the Northern Song Dynasty exceed that in the previous era tremendously. The inscriptions are mostly reign titles. The nine emperors changed their reign titles for 35 times in all, and cast 27 kinds of reign title coins and 3 kinds of non-reign title coins.

The copper coin was the dominating coins in the Northern Song Dynasty, as well as some iron coin were circulating, and in some places, both of them were used at the same time. They were cast finely and beautifully, mainly with the names as *Tongbao, Yuanbao*. The inscription's calligraphy is graceful and mostly written by emperors and famous

御书钱

御书钱是由皇帝亲笔书写钱文的钱币，以北宋铸造的最多。

北宋初年的"淳化元宝"，钱文由宋太宗赵炅书写，是最早出现的御书钱。淳化元宝分楷、行、草三种书体，美名"三书钱"，其楷书微具隶意，稳重苍劲，节奏分明；行书清晰，潇洒秀逸；草书系章草，笔健墨活，自如飞扬。太宗最先采用草书、行书入钱币，为钱文书法艺术开辟了新天地。

公元1101年，宋徽宗赵佶继位，中国的御书钱进入了全盛时期。他的书法称为"瘦金体"，自然窈窕，文采斑斓，如美女簪花。御书钱中以"崇宁通宝""大观通宝"最为精美，是宋徽宗用瘦金体书写的。

Imperial Inscription Money

The imperial inscription money indicates the inscription of the money is written by the emperor himself, which is mainly of the Northern Song Dynasty.

In the early Northern Song Dynasty, the *Chunhua Yuanbao* was written by Emperor Taizong, Zhao Jiong, which was the first imperial inscription money. The *Chunhua Yuanbao* has three calligraphy fonts, *Kai, Xing* and *Cao*, also known as the "three-font money". Its calligraphy of *Kai* is slightly similar to the font *Li*, which is with dignity and strength, as well as clear rhythm; its calligraphy of *Xing* is distinct and elegant; its calligraphy of *Cao* belongs to the *Zhangcao* (a specific calligraphy style of *Cao*), with strong structure and vivid spirit. Emperor Taizong firstly applied the calligraphy fonts of *Cao* and *Xing* in the coin inscription, which created a new world for the inscription calligraphy.

In 1101, Emperor Huizong, Zhao Ji succeeded to the throne. Then the imperial inscription money was in full bloom in China. His calligraphy is called "Thin Gold Style", with natural and graceful body, rich and vivid changes, like a decorated gorgeous beauty. The most exquisite imperial inscription moneys are *Chongning Tongbao and Daguan Tongbao*, which are written by Emperor Huizong with the "Thin Gold Style".

- 崇宁通宝（北宋）
Chongning Tongbao (Northern Song Dynasty, 960-1127)

- 大观通宝（北宋）
Daguan Tongbao (Northern Song Dynasty, 960-1127)

• 宋元通宝（北宋）

宋元通宝边郭较宽，钱文隶书，光背或有星纹、月纹。

Songyuan Tongbao (Northern Song Dynasty, 960-1127)

Songyuan Tongbao has a relatively narrow rim and inscription of font *Li*, blank back or with star or moon patterns.

年号钱。淳化元宝与至道元宝均为宋太宗御书钱。

宋真宗时，铸有"咸平元宝""景德元宝""祥符元宝""祥符通宝""天禧通宝"五种年号钱，均为真书。其中以祥符钱版式较多，有小平、折二、折三、折五、折十数种。

calligraphers, which processes very high artistic value. Among them, the most exquisite ones are founded in the reign of Emperor Huizong, which are the top coins in the Song Dynasty.

In the reign of Emperor Taizong, the government cast *Songyuan Tongbao*, *Taiping Tongbao*, *Chunhua Yuanbao* and *Zhidao Yuanbao*. *Songyuan Tongbao* is *Xiaoping* (little flat) copper or iron coin copyed from the *Zhouyuan Tongbao*, which was the first casting-coin in the Northern Song Dynasty. *Taiping Tongbao* was the first reign title coin in the Northern Song Dynasty. Both *Chunhua Yuanbao* and *Zhidao Yuanbao* are imperial inscription money written by Emperor Taizong.

In the reign of Emperor Zhenzong, the government cast *Xianping Yuanbao*, *Jingde Yuanbao*, *Xiangfu Yuanbao*, *Xiangfu Tongbao*, *Tianxi Tongbao*, five reign title coins, which are all written in the font *Zhen* (font *Kai*). And the *Xiangfu* coin has relatively more formats like *Xiaoping*, *Zhe'er*, *Zhesan*, *Zhewu*, *Zheshi*, etc.

• 祥符元宝（北宋）

Xiangfu Yuanbao (Northern Song Dynasty, 960-1127)

宋仁宗时，铸行的钱币种类较多，有"天圣元宝""明道元宝""景祐元宝""皇宋通宝""康定元宝""庆历重宝""至和元宝""至和通宝""至和重宝""嘉祐元宝""嘉祐通宝"等。

宋英宗时，铸有"治平通宝""治平元宝"铜、铁对钱，钱文书体为楷、篆、古篆三体。

宋神宗时，铸有"熙宁元宝""熙宁通宝""熙宁重宝""元丰通宝""元丰重宝"。其中"元丰通宝""元丰重宝"为铜、铁对钱，钱文书体为篆、隶、行三体。

宋哲宗时，铸有"元祐通宝"、"绍圣元宝""绍圣通宝""绍圣重宝""元符通宝""元符重宝"，均为年号钱。其中"绍圣元宝""绍

In the reign of Emperor Renzong, the casting coins had relatively more kinds, including *Tiansheng Yuanbao, Mingdao Yuanbao, Jingyou Yuanbao, Huangsong Tongbao, Kangding Yuanbao, Qingli Zhongbao, Zhihe Yuanbao, Zhihe Tongbao, Zhihe Zhongbao, Jiayou Yuanbao, Jiayou Tongbao*, etc.

In the reign of Emperor Yingzong, the government cast copper and iron pair money of *Zhiping Tongbao, Zhiping Yuanbao*, with three calligraphy fonts, *Kai, Zhuan* and ancient *Zhuan*.

In the reign of Emperor Shenzong, the government cast *Xining Yuanbao, Xining Tongbao, Xining Zhongbao, Yuanfeng Tongbao*, and *Yuanfeng Zhongbao*. The *Yuanfeng Tongbao* and *Yuanfeng Zhongbao* are copper and iron pair money, with the inscription

• 元丰通宝铁钱母钱（北宋）
Mother-Coin of Iron Money of *Yuanfeng Tongbao* (Northern Song Dynasty, 960-1127)

• 绍圣元宝（北宋）
Shaosheng Yuanbao (Northern Song Dynasty, 960-1127)

圣通宝""绍圣重宝"为铜、铁对钱。

宋徽宗时期，铸钱精绝，居宋钱之冠，有"建国通宝""圣宋元宝""圣宋通宝""崇宁通宝""崇宁重宝""崇宁元宝""大观通宝""政和通宝""政和重宝""重和通宝""宣和通宝""宣和元宝"。

宋钦宗在位时间短，铸钱不多，仅铸有"靖康元宝""靖康通宝"。

此外，北宋淳化年间，王小波、李顺起义，曾铸"应感通宝""应运元宝""应运通宝"等铜、铁小平钱。

calligraphy fonts of *Zhuan*, *Li*, and *Xing*.

In the reign of Emperor Zhezong, the government cast *Yuanyou Tongbao*, *Shaosheng Yuanbao*, *Shaosheng Tongbao*, *Shaosheng Zhongbao*, *Yuanfu Tongbao*, and *Yuanfu Zhongbao*, all of which are reign title money. *Shaosheng Yuanbao*, *Shaosheng Tongbao* and *Shaosheng Zhongbao* are copper or iron pair money.

In the reign of Emperor Huizong, the foundry coins are of the most exquisite quality, which occupy the top position in the Song Dynasty, including *Jianguo Tongbao*, *Shengsong Yuanbao*, *Shengsong Tongbao*, *Chongning Tongbao*, *Chongning Zhongbao*, *Chongning Yuanbao*, *Daguan Tongbao*, *Zhenghe Tongbao*, *Zhenghe Zhongbao*,

- 靖康元宝（北宋）

  Jingkang Yuanbao (Northern Song Dynasty, 960-1127)

- 靖康通宝（北宋）

  Jingkang Tongbao (Northern Song Dynasty, 960-1127)

- 应感通宝（北宋）
Yinggan Tongbao (Northern Song Dynasty, 960-1127)

- 应运元宝（北宋）
Yingyun Yuanbao (Northern Song Dynasty, 960-1127)

- 应运通宝铁钱（北宋）
Iron Money of Yingyun Tongbao (Northern Song Dynasty, 960-1127)

Chonghe Tongbao, Xuanhe Tongbao, and *Xuanhe Yuanbao*.

In the short reign of Emperor Qinzong, the government didn't cast many coins, only the *Jingkang Yuanbao* and *Jingkang Tongbao*.

Besides, in the Chunhua Period of the Northern Song Dynasty, Wang Xiaobo and Li Shun uprose, and once cast copper or iron *Xiaoping* (little flat) coins like *Yinggan Tongbao, Yingyun Yuanbao, Yingyun Tongbao*, etc.

夹锡钱

夹锡钱又称为"铁夹锡""夹锡""夹锡铁钱""锡铁钱""锡钱"等，是北宋末年宰相蔡京力主推行的一种钱币。

北宋实行夹锡钱是因为夹杂铅锡的钱币，脆不可用，能防止辽、西夏将铁钱改熔作兵器。另外，铁钱中增加锡铅成分后，熔点降低了，改善了铁熔液的流动性，铁钱的质量大为提高。这样，统治阶级就利用夹锡钱的成本略高于铁钱这一点，抬高夹锡钱的比价，转移财政危机。

Mixed Tin Money

Mixed tin money is also called as "iron-mixed tin", "mixed tin", "tin-and-iron mixed money", "tin-iron money", "tin money", etc., which the coin promoted by the prime minister Cai Jing of the end of Northern Song Dynasty.

As the led-and-tin mixed coin was too fragile to be used, the Northern Song government decided to use this coin to prevent the Khitan and Tangut melt the iron coins to make weapons. Besides, after adding the tin and led into the iron coins, the melting point was lowered which improved the liquidity of the iron solution and then raised the iron coin's quality greatly. In this way, the ruling class took advantage of the higher cost of the mixed tin money to raise its exchange rate and transfer the financial crisis.

南宋铜铁钱

南宋共有7个皇帝，改了20次年号，共铸18种年号钱和3种非年号钱。

南宋铸币的材质也是铜和铁，但是铜材匮乏，铁钱成为南宋主要的钱币。

南宋铸钱规模和数量远不及北宋，钱背文或记监、记地、记值、记年号年数，铸工精良，钱文书体兼楷、草、隶、篆各体，以楷书为主，极具艺术欣赏价值。

宋高宗时，铸有"建炎通宝""建炎元宝""建炎重宝""绍兴元宝""绍兴通宝"。其中建炎通宝有小平、折二、折三等铜、铁对钱，钱文篆、楷二体，

Copper Coins and Iron Coins in the Southern Song Dynasty (1127-1279)

There were seven emperors in the Southern Song Dynasty who changed their reign titles for 20 times, and totally cast 18 kinds of reign title money and 3 kinds of non-reign title money.

The materials used to cast the coins of the Southern dynasties are also copper and iron. However, due to the shortage of the copper, iron coin became the main currency in this period.

The scale and quantity of the casting coin of the Southern Song Dynasty were nowhere near as much as those of the Northern Song dynasties. The back inscriptions are marked by the supervisor, location, value or the reign title, with fine and exquisite quality. The fonts of

铸量较多，版别复杂，有大、小字之分。

宋孝宗时，铸有"隆兴元宝""隆兴通宝""乾道元

● 建炎元宝（南宋）
Jianyan Yuanbao (Southern Song Dynasty, 1127-1279)

● 建炎通宝（南宋）
Jianyan Tongbao (Southern Song Dynasty, 1127-1279)

the coin inscriptions include *Kai, Cao, Li, Zhuan*, mainly in *Kai*, which process high artistic value.

In the reign of Emperor Gaozong, the government cast *Jianyan Tongbao, Jianyan Yuanbao, Jianyan Zhongbao, Shaoxing Yuanbao, Shaoxing Tongbao*, among which, the *Jianyan Tongbao* has several kinds of copper and iron pair money like *Xiaoping, Zhe'er, Zhesan*, etc., with two fonts of inscription as *Zhuan, Kai*, of a large quantity and complex versions, and varies in the size of the characters.

记年钱和记监钱

记年钱指钱币背面标明具体铸造年份的钱币。从汉武帝刘彻登基称建元元年（前140年）开始，就以帝王年号为记年。记年钱在南宋时才出现，南宋淳熙七年（1180年）铸造的"淳熙元宝"，背文有"柒"字记年，是中国最早出现的记年钱。记年钱的出现是钱币史上的一个进步，通过钱文就可以知道铸钱年代。钱币记年制度也一直沿用到宋末，成为宋代钱币的一个特点。

记监钱指钱背标有钱监或钱局（铸造钱币机构名称）的钱币。记地钱到南宋发展

● 绍熙通宝铁钱母钱（南宋）
Mother Coin of Iron Money of *Shaoxi Tongbao* (Southern Song Dynasty, 1127-1279)

成为记监钱，如南宋的乾道元宝，背文"同"字，为舒州同安监所铸；绍熙通宝，背文"汉"字，为湖北汉阳监所铸。

此外，还有些钱币记监兼记年。如南宋宁宗庆元年间铸造的庆元通宝，背文有"同元""春二""汉三"等多种。"同元"意为庆元元年间，同安监铸造；"春二"意为庆元二年间，蕲春监铸造；"汉三"意为庆元三年间，汉阳监铸造。

- 庆元通宝（南宋）
  Qingyuan Tongbao (Southern Song Dynasty, 1127-1279)

Year Money and Supervisor Money

The year money indicates the coin with its back inscribed the specific casting year. Ever since Emperor Wu of the Han Dynasty, Liu Che, succeeded the throne in 140 B.C., and proclaimed this year as the 1st year of Jianyuan (his reign title), the central government recorded the year with the emperor's reign title. The year money didn't emerge until the Southern Song Dynasty. In 1180 (7th year of Hongxi), the year money *Hongxi Yuanbao* was cast, with a character " 柒 (seven)" at the back to mark the year, which is the first year money in China. The birth of year money is a progress on the currency history. Acccording to the coins, the casting year can be told. And the system was also passed down by the end of the Song Dynasty, which became a feature of the coins in that period of time.

The supervisor money indicates the coin with its back inscribed the name of the money inspection institution or the foundry office (the agency where people cast coins). The location money became the supervisor money by the Southern Song Dynasty, like the *Qiandao Yuanbao* with the character " 同 " at the back referring to its foundry office, Tong'an Inspection Instituion of Shuzhou and the *Shaoxi Tongbao*, with the character " 汉 " at the back referring to its foundry office, Hanyang Inspection Institution of Hubei.

Besides, there are several coins marked both by the supervisor and casting year, like the *Qingyuan Tongbao* cast in the Qingyuan Period of the Southern Song Dynasty, with *Tongyuan, Chun'er, Hansan*, etc. *Tongyuan* indicates the casting year is the 1st year of the Qingyuan Period, and the foundry office, Tong'an Inspection Institution; *Chun'er* indicates the casting year is the 2nd year of the Qingyuan Period, and the foundry office, Qichun Inspection Institution; *Hansan* indicates the casting year is the 3rd year of the Qingyuan Period, and the foundry office, Hanyang Inspection Instituion.

宝""乾道通宝""淳熙元宝""淳熙通宝"。其中淳熙元宝背铸"柒"字,是中国最早出现的记年钱。

宋光宗时,铸有"绍熙元宝""绍熙通宝"铜、铁钱,背文记年。

宋宁宗时,铸有"庆元元宝""庆元通宝""嘉泰元宝""嘉泰通宝""开禧元宝""开禧通宝""嘉定元宝""嘉定通宝""圣宋重宝"等,背文多记年、记监。

宋理宗时,铸有"宝庆元宝""大宋通宝""大宋元宝""绍定元宝""绍定通宝""端平元宝""端平通宝""端平重宝""嘉熙通

In the reign of Emperor Xiaozong, the government cast *Longxing Yuanbao, Longxing Tongbao, Qiandao Yuanbao, Qiandao Tongbao, Chunxi Yuanbao, Chunxi Tongbao*. Among them, the *Chunxi Yuanbao* with a character " 柒 " (Qi, seven) carved at its back, which is the earliest year money in China.

In the reign of Emperor Guangzong, the government cast copper and iron coins like *Shaoxi Yuanbao* and *Shaoxi Tongbao*, with the casting year marked at back.

In the reign of Emperor Ningzong, the government cast *Qingyuan Yuanbao, Jiatai Yuanbao, Jiatai Tongbao, Kaixi Yuanbao, Kaixi Tongbao, Jiading Yuanbao, Jiading Tongbao, Shengsong Zhongbao*, etc., mostly with the casting

• 嘉泰元宝铁钱母钱(南宋)
Mother Coin of the Iron Money of *Jiatai Yuanbao* (Southern Song Dynasty, 1127-1279)

• 开禧通宝(南宋)
Kaixi Tongbao (Southern Song Dynasty, 1127-1279)

• 嘉定通宝铁钱母钱（南宋）
Mother Coin of the Iron Money of *Jiading Tongbao* (Southern Song Dynasty, 1127-1279)

宝""嘉熙重宝""淳祐元宝""淳祐通宝""皇宋元宝""开庆通宝""景定元宝"，背文多记年、记监。

宋度宗时，铸有"咸淳元宝"，背文记年，是南宋最后一种年号钱。

year and inspection institution's name marked at back.

In the reign of Emperor Lizong, the government cast *Baoqing Yuanbao, Dasong Yuanbao, Shaoding Yuanbao, Shaoding Tongbao, Duanping Yuanbao, Duanping Tongbao, Duanping Zhongbao, Jiaxi Tongbao, Jiaxi Zhongbao, Chunyou Yuanbao, Chunyou Tongbao, Huangsong Yuanbao, Kaiqing Tongbao, Jingding Yuanbao*, mostly with the casting year and inspection institution carved at back.

In the reign of Emperor Duzong, the government cast *Xianchun Yuanbao*, with the casting year carved at back, which is the last year money in the Southern Song Dynasty.

钱牌

南宋时期，经济得到了长足发展，铜钱时常供不应求，不能满足市场的需求，出现钱荒现象。为了维持正常的商业活动，朝廷明令禁止铜钱出城。此令一经颁布，临安城内外只得依赖纸币进行贸易流通。而大额纸币有不便找零的弊端，于是就出现了行使代币职能的钱牌。

钱牌又称"铜牌"，长方形，额部铸有小孔，可穿系，方便携带，上下两角形制为长方形，有铜、铅两种材质。面文"临安府行用"标示铸行地域，背文为"准贰伯文省""准叁伯文省""准伍伯文省"注明折值，面背均有较为浅显的边郭，传世少见。（"准"意为"平"，"伯"通"佰"，"省"当"省佰"讲）

南宋钱牌多在杭州一带流通，如临安府钱牌只限于在临安府流通。

Money Plate

In the Southern Song Dynasty, with the great economic development, the demand for the copper coin exceeded the supply from time to time. The cast coin couldn't meet the market demand and led to the great shortage of money. In order to maintain the regular business activities, the courtyard banned the copper coin circulating out of the palace. Once the order was issued, people could only rely on the paper money to trade with each other. And the large bills are not easy to be changed into small amount, so the money plate appeared to play the function of token money.

Money plate also called as "copper plate", with rectangle shape and a small hole at the head for stringing together and being carried on. And the upper and lower corners are formed in rectangle. It's made from two kinds of materials copper and led, with facial inscription "used in Lin'an" to indicate the casting location, and the back inscription *Zhun Erbaiwen Sheng, Zhun Sanbaiwen Sheng , Zhun Wubaiwen Sheng* (*Zhun* means flat; *Bai* means hundred, *Sheng* means *being equivalent to one hundred*) to indicate its value. There are light rims along the facial and back sides. And it is rarely seen at present day.

The money plate of the Southern Song Dynasty was mainly circulated around Hangzhou. For instance, the money plate of Lin'an was only circulated in the Lin'an.

临安府钱牌（南宋）

钱牌带有穿孔，方便携带。牌面文为"临安府行用"，牌背文为"准肆拾文省"。

Money Plate of Lin'an (Southern Song Dynasty, 1127-1279)

The money plate has a small hole for carrying on, with facial inscription of "used in Lin'an", and back inscription of *Zhun Sishiwen Sheng*.

金银铸币

宋代金银钱较唐代更为盛行，不仅保留了唐代宫廷赏赐金银的习惯，而且还明确规定允许私人铸造金银钱。同时金银钱也进入流通，可以用来购买物资。另外，宋代佛教、道教都很活跃，曾铸造过不少金银"供养钱"，如"淳化元宝"佛像金钱。

银铤

宋代银铤是由唐代束腰形银铤发展而来的。

北宋银铤有三种基本形制：一是平首，微束腰，面大于底；二是

"淳化元宝"佛像金钱（北宋）
Buddha Gold Coin *Chunhua Yuanbao* (Northern Song Dynasty, 960-1127)

Gold and Silver Casting Coins

The gold and silver casting coins were more popular than the ones of Tang Dynasty (618-907). On one hand, it preserved the the habit of awading gold and silver in the courtyard of Tang Dynasty, on the other hand, the Buddism and Taoism greatly prevailed in the Song Dynasty, so many gold and silver worship coins were cast, like the Buddha gold coin *Chunhua Yuanbao*.

Silver *Ding*

Silver *Ding* of the Song Dynasty is developed from the girdling-shaped silver *Ding* of the Tang Dynasty (618-907).

The silver *Ding* of Nothern Song Dynasty has three basic forms: one is with flat head, slightly tightened up waist, larger surface than the bottom; one is with arched head, tightened up waist, slightly bulging belly; one is with round head, tightened up waist, slightly bulging belly. All of these three forms have complex carving and inscriptions, basically with the value of 50 *Liang* (2.5 kg), with the real weight of 2 kg.

The silver *Ding* of the Southern Song Dynasty is with the form of arched head, tightened up waist, and thicker head than the waist, indented in the middle of the Ding's surface, and ripples or protruding

- 十二两半的银铤（南宋）
Silver *Ding* of Twelve *Liang* and A Half (Southern Song Dynasty, 1127-1279)

- "苏宅韩五郎"金铤（南宋）
Gold *Ding* of *Suzhai Hanwulang* (Southern Song Dynasty, 1127-1279)

弧首，束腰，中部微凹；三是圆首，束腰，中央微凹。这三种形制的银铤，均有内容复杂的錾刻或钤盖的铭文，基本为五十两，实重约2000克。

南宋银铤的形制为弧首、束腰形，首部厚于腰部，铤面中央内凹，四周有波纹或凸棱，錾刻或钤盖内容复杂的铭文，有五十两、二十五两、十二两半三种规格。

金铤和金牌

金铤和金牌是南宋时期铸行的黄金称量货币。其形制为长方薄片形，重约4克（相当于宋制的一钱），铸有"十分金""赤金""界内""河东""石元铺""马丁家""张二郎"等铭文，代表黄金成色、区域、金银铺号、工匠姓名，以及金银铺号的押记等。

ridges around. It's carved with complex inscriptions, with three norms of fifty *Liang*, twenty-five *Liang*, twelve *Liang* and a half.

Gold *Ding* and Gold Plate

The gold *Ding* and gold plate were the gold weighing currency cast in the Southern Song Dynasty, with a shape of thin rectangle and a weight of 4g (equals to 1 *Qian* according to the Song criterion), carved with *Shifenjin*, *Chijin*, *Jienei*, *Hedong*, *Shiyuanpu*, *Madingjia*, *Zhang'erlang*, etc., representing the gold's percentage, location, the gold shop name, craftsman's name, the mortgage record of the gold shop, etc.

Paper Currency

The paper currency was greatly promoted in the Song Dynasty. *Jiaozi* was evolved from the flying money in the Tang

纸币

宋代是纸币获得推广的重要时期。在唐代飞钱的基础上演变而来的"交子"产生,率先在当时较为发达的四川地区流通,继而又产生了以铜钱为本位币的"会子"。

交子

交子产生于民间,经历了由民间私设的私交子到官办的官交子的发展过程。私交子是一种可兑换的信用货币,采用同一纸张,同一版式印刷,统一发行,根据收入现钱贯数临时填写面额,每交面额一

Dynasty and firstly circulated in the relatively well-developed Sichuan area. And then *Huizi* was born, which used copper coin as its standard money.

Jiaozi

Jiaozi was firstly used among the folks. It had been through the development from the private money to the official currency. Private *Jiaozi* is an exchangeable credit currency, adopting the same paper, same format to print, and is issued uniformly. It's according to the income quantity of the *Guan* to fill in its value temporarily. Each *Jiao* values one *Guan*; and three-year makes one extent. While exchanging, each *Guan* should pay 30 *Wen* as the cost of the paper and ink. Later, this private *Jiaozi* brought about credit crisis. In 1023, Emperor Renzong set the *Jiaozi* Agency in Yizhou. Since then *Jiaozi* was issued by the government and became the legal tender circulated in the areas of Sichuan, Shaanxi, Hedong

- 交子(北宋)

Jiaozi (Northern Song Dynasty, 960-1127)

贯，三年为一界。兑现时，每贯扣下三十文，作为纸墨费。后来，这种私交子的信用产生危机。宋仁宗天圣元年（1023年），设益州交子务，交子由官府经营发行，成为法定货币，在四川、陕西、河东（今山西一带）流通。官交子用红、青（蓝）、黑三色铜版套印，印有花押和密码，加盖本州州印，面额固定，流通期限以三年为界，界满更换新的。

北宋徽宗崇宁四年（1105年），交子被强制推行到大部分地区通用，并改称"钱引"。

(present Shanxi Province). The official *Jiaozi* was overprinted by the three-color (red, blue and black) copper board and was printed with signs and codes, and was stamped with the local official seals, with fixed value and three-year circulating time limit. When expiring, it should be changed into new one.

In 1105, *Jiaozi* was mandatorily carried out to the most part of China, and changed its name into "guiding money".

钱引

钱引，亦称"川引"，作为兑换钱币的凭证，流通于四川外诸路，以铁钱计价，引上印有面额、界分及年限等，并配有各种图案花纹。钱引的花纹图案，印有红、蓝、黑三种颜色，是中国最早的带色纸币。钱引面额有五百文、一贯两种，初以两年为一界进行换发，后来增为三年为一界，甚至十年一界。钱引最终因为不能兑现而严重贬值。

南宋时，钱引仍在继续流通。南宋理宗宝祐四年（1256年），朝廷收回了四川纸币印造权，在四川地区印行会子。

Guiding Money

Guiding money, also known as "Guiding *Chuan*", as a receipt of money exchange, circulating round Sichuan area, is valued by iron money, with value, extent, and age limit, as well as several motifs and patterns which are printed in three colors: red, blue and black. It is the earliest colored banknote in China, with the value of 500 *Wen* and 1 *Guan*, two kinds. At first, it was issued and changed in every two years, later, in every three years, even in every ten years. As guiding money can not be cashed, it was eventually depreciated severely.

In the Southern Song Dynasty, guiding money was still in the circulation. In 1256, the courtyard took back the paper money printing authority from Sichuan, and printed *Huizi* in this area instead.

会子

会子又称"便钱会子",是南宋最主要的纸币。初由商办,作为汇票、支票之类的票据。宋高宗绍兴三十年(1160年)改为官办,成为兼有流通职能的铜钱兑换券。

会子形制为长方形,面额有一贯、二百文、三百文、五百文等,一贯为一会,三年为一界,面文有篆体字的面额(一贯文省)、故事图(张良纳履故事)、专典官押(三字)、字号、朱印三颗。会子比交子流通区域更广、发行数量更多。

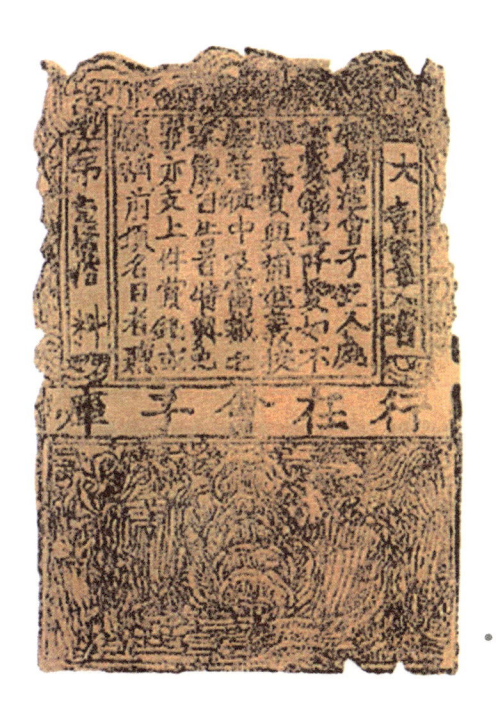

Huizi

Huizi, also known as "convenient money *Huizi*", was the main banknote in the Southern Song Dynasty. At first, it was created by the businessman, and used as bills like draft and check. In 1160, it was issued by the government, and became the exchange certificate of copper money with circulation function.

Huizi is in rectangle shape, with the value of 1 *Guan*, 200 *Wen*, 300 *Wen*, 500 *Wen*, etc. 1 *Guan* equals to 1 *Hui*; and three-year is one limit. The facial inscription printed with the value in the font *Zhuan* (*Yiguanwen Sheng*), stories (the story of *Zhang Liang Wearing Shoes*), the official signs (in three characters), the name of the shop and three red seals. *Huizi* was circulated in broader areas and was issued in larger quantity than *Jiaozi*.

- 会子(南宋)
  Huizi (Southern Song Dynasty, 1127-1279)

关子

关子最初只是一种兑换票据，类似唐代的飞钱。后来发展成为南宋流通纸币，有见钱关子、铜钱关子、金银关子、公田关子等。关子除作为纸币外，还有作为榷场发给商人的运销凭证、税务部门发给出口商人的货物纳税凭证等用途。

Guanzi

Guanzi was originally an exchange bill, similar to the flying money of the Tang Dynasty. Later, it was developed into the circulating banknote in the Southern Song Dynasty, including *Jianqian Guanzi*, copper-coin *Guanzi*, gold-and-silver *Guanzi*, *Gongtian Guanzi*, etc. Except for being banknote, *Guanzi* also can be used as the selling certificate issued in the *Quechang* (market), or the tax payment receipt of the export goods issued by the revenue department.

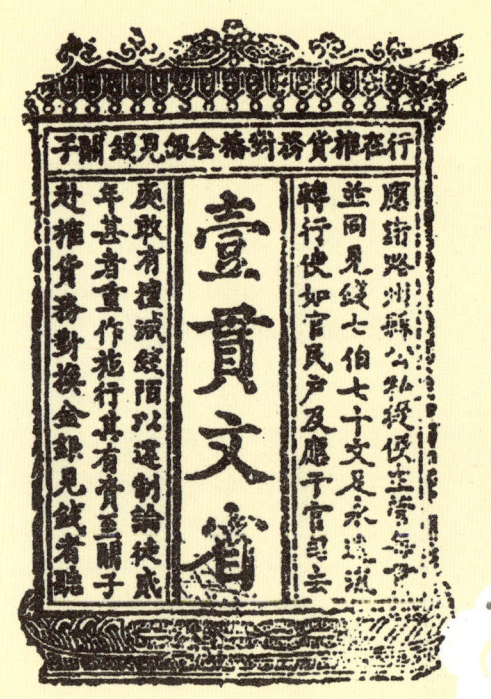

- 关子（南宋）
  Guanzi (Southern Song Dynasty, 1127-1279)

> 辽、西夏、金代钱币

辽代钱币

辽是北方游牧民族契丹族建立的少数民族政权。辽代钱币铸造数量较少，铸工粗糙，钱背常常错范。钱文多是汉文，旋读，文字不精美，书体为隶兼八分，有时一枚钱上有两种字体，笔意古拙，极富特色，没有对钱。在钱文、形制上，具有明显的传承性。辽代钱币早期受五代钱币影响，后期多受宋代钱币影响，最终确立了货币制度，流通的货币多是小平钱。

据说，契丹族在改国号为辽之前，就铸有钱币。如"开丹圣宝""天朝万顺""通行泉货""丹巡贴宝""千秋万岁"

> Currencies of the Liao Dynasty (907-1125), Western Xia Dynasty (1038-1227) and Jin Dynasty (1115-1234)

Currencies of the Liao Dynasty (907-1125)

The Liao Dynasty was an authority which was set by the northern nomadic people, Khitan. The casting coin of the Liao Dynasty is in small quantity and rough technique. The coin back was often cast staggered. The inscriptions are mainly written in Han language, and read in revolving order, with scratchy handwriting and the font of *Li* and *Bafen*, sometimes carved with both of them in the same coin. The calligraphy is rough yet distinctive. It didn't have the pair money. In the inscription and forms, it has obvious lineage. The early stage of the

- 天朝万顺（辽）

钱文为契丹文"天朝万顺"。
Tianchao Wanshun (Liao Dynasty, 907-1125)

The inscription is written in Khitan as *Tianchao Wanshun*.

- 通行泉货（辽）

Tongxing Quanhuo (Liao Dynasty, 907-1125)

等。在改国号为辽之后，辽代所铸的钱币多为年号钱。

辽太祖耶律阿保机在天赞年间，铸有"天赞通宝"；辽太宗天显年间，铸有"天显通宝"；辽世宗天禄元年（947年），铸造"天禄通宝"；辽穆宗应历元年（951年），铸造"应历通宝"；辽景宗保宁年间，铸有"保宁通宝"；辽圣宗统

coins of Liao Dynasty was inuenced by the ones of the Five dynasties (907-960); and the later stage was affected by the coins of the Song Dynasty. It established the monetary system and the circulated currencies were mainly the *Xiaoping* (little and flat) Coins.

It's said, before the Khitan changed their dynasty title to the "Liao", they had already cast coins, like *Kaidan Shengbao, Tianchao Wanshun, Tongxing Quanhuo, Danxun Tiebao, Qianqiu Wansui,* etc. After they changed the title into Liao, the foundry coin of the Liao Dynasty was mainly the reign title money.

Emperor Taizu of Liao, Yelv Abaoji, during the Tianzan Period (922-925), cast the *Tianzan Tongbao*; Emperor Taizong of Liao, during the Tianxian Period (926-937), cast the *Tianxian Tongbao*; Emperor Shizong of Liao, in the 1st year of the Tianlu Period (947), cast *Tianlu Tongbao*; Emperor Muzong of Liao, in the 1st year of the Yingli Period (951), cast *Yingli Tongbao*; Emperor Jingzong of Liao, during the Baoning Period (969-979), cast *Baoning Tongbao*; Emperor Shengzong of Liao, in the 1st year of the Tonghe Period (983), cast *Tonghe Yuanbao*; Emperor Xingzong of Liao, during the Chongxi Period (1032-1055),

和元年（983年），铸造"统和元宝"；辽兴宗重熙年间，铸有"重熙通宝"。

辽道宗在位46年用了5个年号，即清宁、咸雍、大康、大安、寿昌，铸有"清宁通宝""咸雍通宝""大康元宝""大康通宝""大安元宝""寿昌元宝"。辽末年，天祚帝时，铸有"乾统元宝""天庆元宝""大辽天庆"。

cast *Chongxi Zhongbao*.

Emperor Daozong of Liao ruled the country for 46 years (1055-1101), changed 5 reign titles, which are Qingning, Xianyong, Dakang, Da'an, Shouchang, and cast *Qingning Tongbao, Xianyong Tongbao, Dakang Yuanbao, Dakang Tongbao, Da'an Yuanbao, Shouchang Yuanbao* respectively. In the late Liao Dynasty, Emperor Tianzuo, cast *Qiantong Yuanbao, Tianqing Yuanbao,* and *Daliao Tianqing*.

- 清宁通宝（辽）
Qingning Tongbao (Liao Dynasty, 907-1125)

- 咸雍通宝（辽）
Xianyong Tongbao (Liao Dynasty, 907-1125)

- 大康元宝（辽）
Dakang Yuanbao (Liao Dynasty, 907-1125)

- 大康通宝（辽）
Dakang Tongbao (Liao Dynasty, 907-1125)

- 乾统元宝（辽）
Qiantong Yuanbao (Liao Dynasty, 907-1125)

西夏钱币

西夏是由党项族于1038年建立的一个少数民族政权。党项族是羌族的一支，是一个古老的民族。西夏流通中的货币仍以宋代钱币为主，西夏铸钱不多，但铸造精良，钱文书体端庄，多为年号钱。根据钱文的不同可分为西夏文钱和汉文钱两种。西夏文钱币的铸行早于西夏汉文钱币，具有浓厚的民族特色，铸量较少，存世罕见，后来汉文钱和西夏文钱并铸。西夏仁宗天盛之后，只铸造汉文钱，并铸有铁钱。

西夏文钱

西夏文钱的铸行早于西夏汉文钱，铸量较少，存世罕见，现知的只有五种：西夏毅宗福盛承道元年（1053年）所铸的"福圣宝钱"、西夏惠宗大安元年（1074年）所铸的"大安宝钱"、西夏崇宗贞观元年（1101年）所铸的"贞观宝钱"、西夏仁宗乾祐元年（1170年）所铸的"乾祐宝钱"、西夏桓宗天庆元年（1194年）所铸的"天庆宝钱"。

西夏汉文钱

西夏汉文钱也均为年号钱，大

Currencies of the Western Xia Dynasty (1038-1227)

The Western Xia Dynasty was an authority which was established by the Tangut in 1038. The Tangut is an ancient ethnic group which is a branch of the Qiang group. The currencies circulated in the Western Xia were maily the ones of the Song Dynasty. The government itself didn't cast many coins, however, the technique was excellent and the inscription was elegant, mostly were reign title coins. Accroding to the differences of the inscriptions, it can be divided into the ones with the Western Xia language and the ones with the Han language. The former type was cast earlier than the latter one, possessing strong ethnical features, with little casting quantity and rarely being seen at present. Later, the two types of money were cast at the same time. After the Tiansheng Period, they only cast the coins with the Han language, as well as the iron money.

Coin with Western Xia Language

The coin with Western Xia language was founded earlier than the one with Han language, with little casting quantity and rarely being seen at present. The existing five kinds are as below: in the 1st year

乾祐元宝（西夏）
Qianyou Yuanbao (Western Xia Dynasty, 1038-1227)

概有六个年号铸有西夏汉文钱。西夏崇宗元德年间铸"元德通宝""元德重宝"；西夏仁宗天盛年间铸"天盛元宝"；西夏仁宗乾祐年间铸"乾祐元宝"；西夏桓宗天庆元年（1194年）铸"天庆元宝"；西夏襄宗皇建元年（1210年）铸"皇建元宝"；西夏神宗光定元年（1211年）铸"光定元宝"。

金代钱币

金代是中国东北地区的女真族在1115年建立的少数民族政权。金代钱币货币种类繁多，受南宋钱币的影响，铜钱、纸币、白银共同流通。建国初，使用辽代和宋代铜钱。到海陵

of the Fusheng Chengdao Period (1053), Emperor Yizong cast *Fusheng Baoqian*; in the 1st year of the Da'an Period (1074), Emperor Huizong cast *Da'an Baoqian*, in the 1st year of the Zhenguan Period (1101), Emperor Chongzhen cast *Zhenguan Baoqian*, in the 1st year of the Qianyou Period (1170), Emperor Renzong cast *Qianyou Baoqian*, in the 1st year of the Tianqing Period (1194), Emperor Huanzong cast *Tianqing Baoqian*.

Coin with Han Language

The coins with Han language were reign title money, and might be cast in six periods. During the Yuande Period (1119-1126), Emperor Chongzong cast *Yuande Tongbao* and *Yuande Zhongbao*; during the Tiansheng Period (1149-1169), Emperor Renzong cast *Tiansheng Yuanbao*; during the Qianyou Period (1170-1193), Emperor Renzong cast *Qianyou Yuanbao*; in the 1st year of the Tianqing Period (1194), Emperor Huanzong cast *Tianqing Yuanbao*; in the 1st year of the Huangjian Period (1210), Emperor Xiangzong cast *Huangjian Yuanbao*; in the 1st year of the Guangding Period (1211), Emperor Shenzong cast *Guangding Yuanbao*.

王完颜亮时，开始印纸钞，并自铸铜钱，同时还有白银流通。

铜钱

金人掌握了宋代的铸钱工艺，所铸钱币以精美著称。虽然金人有自己的文字，但金代所有钱币的钱文均为汉字，钱文书法十分考究。但限于铜资源的缺乏，铸钱数量不多。

金熙宗皇统元年（1141年），铸"皇统元宝"，存世仅一枚，极为珍贵。海陵王正隆三年（1158年），铸"正隆元宝"，此钱中有一种"正"字末笔长于第四笔，称为"五笔正隆"。金世宗大定十八年（1178年），铸"大定通宝"，钱文仿瘦金体，铸工精美，背多铸

- 大定通宝（金）
Dading Tongbao (Jin Dynasty, 1115-1234)

Currencies of the Jin Dynasty (1115-1234)

The Jin Dynasty was an authority of ethnic group which was established by the Jurchen in 1115. The coins of this dynasty varied in kinds and was influenced by the ones of the Southern Song Dynasty to let the copper money, banknote, silver ingot circulating at the same time. In the early stage, they used the copper coins of the Liao Dynasty and Song Dynasty. By the reign of the King Hailing, Wanyan Liang, the government started to print banknote and cast their own copper coins. Meanwhile, the silver ingot was put into the circulating field.

Copper Money

People of the Jin Dynasty learned the casting techniques from the Song Dynasty. So their coins were famous for their beauty and fineness. Although they had their own characters, the money inscriptions were written in Han language by excellent calligraphy. Due to the shortage of the copper, the foundry coins were in little quantity.

In the 1st year of the Huangtong Period (1141), Emperor Xizong of Jin cast *Huangtong Yuanbao*, which was passed down by only one single piece.

有"申""酉"二字。金章宗泰和四年（1204年），铸"泰和通宝"和"泰和重宝"。卫绍王崇庆元年（1212年），铸"崇庆通宝"和"崇庆元宝"；至宁元年（1213年），铸"至宁元宝"。金宣宗贞祐年间，铸"贞祐元宝"和"贞祐通宝"。

- 泰和通宝（金）
Taihe Tongbao (Jin Dynasty, 1115-1234)

In the 3rd year of the Zhenglong Period (1158), the King Hailing cast *Zhenglong Yuanbao*, which have one kind of coin with its inscription character "正" (*Zheng*) written as the last stroke was longer than the fourth stroke, called as "five-stroke *Zhenglong*". In the 18th year of the Dading Period (1178), Emperor Shizong cast *Dading Tongbao*, which was beautifully cast and with its inscription imitating the "Thin Gold Style" and its back mainly carved by *Shen* and *You*. In the 4th year of the Taihe Period (1204), Emperor Zhangzong cast *Taihe Tongbao* and *Taihe Zhongbao*. In the 1st year of the Chongqing Period (1212), the King Weishao cast *Chongqing Tongbao* and *Chongqing Yuanbao*; in the 1st year of the Zhining Period (1213), the government cast *Zhining Yuanbao*. During the Zhenyou Period (1213-1217), Emperor Xuanzong cast *Zhenyou Yuanbao* and *Zhenyou Tongbao*.

- 泰和重宝（金）

"泰和重宝"的钱文书体为玉箸篆，是著名书法家党怀英所书，秀美典雅，堪称一绝。

Taihe Zhongbao (Jin Dynasty, 1115-1234)

The inscription of *Taihe Zhongbao* applied the font of *Yuzhu Zhuan*, which was created and written by the famous calligrapher Dang Huaiying, with elegant and graceful style.

纸币

金代纸币种类繁多,海陵王贞元二年(1154年)发行的"交钞",是金代最早的纸币。后来从贞祐三年至天兴二年十八年间,出现了"贞祐宝券""贞祐通宝""兴定宝泉""元光重宝""元光珍宝""天兴宝会"等纸币品种。

贞祐三年(1215年),交钞改为"贞祐宝券",不久便贬值成几文钱一贯。兴定元年(1217年),又发行纸币"贞祐通宝",一贯可当一千贯贞祐宝券,一两白银可买

- 贞祐宝券五贯钞版(金)
Money Plate of Five *Guan* of *Zhenyou Baoquan* (Jin Dynasty, 1115-1234)

Paper Money

The paper money varied in kinds in the Jin Dynasty. The *Jiaochao* was issued in the 2nd year of the Zhenyuan Period by the King Hailing was the earliest paper money in the Jin Dynasty. Later, during the Zhenyou Period to the Tianxing Period (1215-1233), the banknots like *Zhenyou Baoquan, Zhenyou Tongbao, Xingding Baoquan, Yuanguang Zhongbao, Yuanguang Zhenbao, Tianxing Baohui*, etc., appeared in these 18 years.

In the 3rd year of the Zhenyou Period (1215), the *Jiaochao* was changed as *Zhenyou Baoquan*, and then after a while, was depreciated into several *Wen* as one *Guan*. In the 1st year of the Xingding Period (1217), it issued the paper money *Zhenyou Tongbao,* as one *Guan* equaled to one thousand *Guan* of the *Zhenyou Baoquan*, and one *Liang* of the silver ingot could buy four *Guan* of the *Zhenyou Tongbao*. Five years later, it was depreciated severely as one *Liang* of the silver ingot could buy eight hundred *Guan* of the *Zhenyou Tonbao*. In the 1st year of the Yuanguang Period (1222), it issued *Xingding Baoquan* which was circulated with *Zhenyou Tongbao* at the same time. In 1223, it issued *Yuanguang*

四贯贞祐通宝，但五年后，也严重贬值，一两白银可买八百余贯贞祐通宝。元光元年（1222年），发行"兴定宝泉"，与贞祐通宝并行。元光二年（1223年），发行"元光重宝"；同年，又发行以"绫"印制的绫币"元光珍宝"。金哀宗天兴二年（1233年），在蔡州发行金代最后的纸币"天兴宝会"，以银两为单位，面值有一钱、二钱、三钱、四钱四种。很快，随着金朝的灭亡，天兴宝会也消失了。

Zhongbao; in the same year, it issued the silk money *Yuanguang Zhenbao*. In the 2nd year of the Tianxing Period (1233), Emperor Aizong cast the last banknote of the Jin Dynasty *Tianxing Baohui* in Caizhou, with the *Liang* as its unit, and with the value of 1 *Qian*, 2 *Qian*, 3 *Qian*, and 4 *Qian*. Soon, with the perishment of the Jin Dynasty, the Tianxing Baohui disappeared too.

交钞

交钞在金代通行长达60年，与铜钱并行流通。交钞是由金统一印制，分路管辖发行的，七年一界，有大、小两种形制。大钞面额有十贯、五贯、四贯、三贯、二贯、一贯等；小钞面额有七百、五百、三百、二百、一百五等。

交钞最初仅在黄河以南地区发行，其目的在于吸纳宋钱。到金世宗大定二十九年（1189年）以后，其界期被取消，可以无期限流通，此后很快就贬值，到宣宗时，几乎贬为废纸。

交钞外围有花栏，上端横书面额，左书字料，右书字号。花栏外围篆书"伪造交钞者斩，告捕者赏钱三百贯"字样；花栏下部印有发行机关地区、赏格、年月日以及各级负责人的押印等；花栏右边有说明每张纸币的工墨费及以旧换新的手续费等文字；左边五行宋体斜文指南京、中都等五个流通区域。迄今为止，尚未发现交钞的纸币实物，只发现了多件印版。

• 壹拾贯交钞版（金）
Printing Plate of *Jiaochao* of Ten *Guan* (Jin Dynasty, 1115-1234)

Jiaochao

Jiaochao was circulated with copper coins in the Jin Dynasty for 60 years, which was printed by the government and issued by the local authorities, with a limit of seven-year and having two forms of large and small versions. The large bill is with the nominal value of 10 *Guan*, 5 *Guan*, 4 *Guan*, 3 *Guan*, 2 *Guan*, 1 *Guan*, etc, while the small bill is with the nominal value of 700, 500, 300, 200, 100, etc.

In the early stage, *Jiaochao* was only issued in the southern areas of the Yellow River, in order to absorb the money of the Song Dynasty. After the year 1189, the limit time was canceled. So the money could circulate without boundries. Soon it started to be depreciated and by the reign of Emperor Xuanzong, its nominal value almost equaled to waste paper.

There was a column printed along the rim of *Jiaochao*, with its value written at the top in horizontal order, and with its *Ziliao* written on the left and its shop name (*Zihao*) written on the right. Outside the column, there was words "for the one who forge the *Jiaochao* beheaded, for the one who report and catch the forger awarded 300 *Guan*" written in *Zhuan*; below the column, it was printed the names of the issue agency and location, the size of a reward, date, and the signatures of the principals of each levels; on the right of the column, it's written the cost of the paper and ink and the commission charge for changing from old ones; on the left of the column, the words written in the italic *Wuxing* Song style indicating the five circulation areas like Nanjing, Zhongdu, etc. So far, the entity of the paper currency (*Jiaochao*) hasn't been found yet, only several printing plates were discovered.

银铤

金章宗时期，随着纸币的贬值，纸币制度遭到严重破坏，同时铜钱匮乏。为化解财政危机，完善货币制度，金章宗于承安二年（1197年）推行新的币制改革，铸行"承安宝货"银铤，作为金代的法定货币，这是中国钱币史上第一次铸造的法定计数白银货币。

"承安宝货"银铤分为一两、

Silver Ding

In the reign of Emperor Zhangzong, with the depreciation of the banknote, the currency system of the paper money was sabotaged and then ran up against the depreciation of the copper coin. In order to resolve the financial crisis and perfect the currency system, Emperor Zhangzong carried out a new currency reform in the 2nd year of the Cheng'an Period (1197) and cast the silver *Ding* of Cheng'an

• 承安宝货银铤（金）
Silver *Ding* of Cheng'an Baohuo (Jin Dynasty, 1115-1234)

一两半、二两半、五两和十两五个等级，每两折钱二贯。银铤钱文为：上首横列"承安"二字，其下右侧直列"宝货壹两"（或"宝货壹两半"），左侧直列"库×部×""库""部"等字，并錾刻不同的押记。目前，所见"承安宝货"银铤有一两（重约40克）和一两半（重约60克），均呈弧首束腰形，含银量95%以上。承安五年（1200年），由于民间纷纷私铸掺杂铜锡的"承安宝货"银铤，于是"承安宝货"银铤停铸。

Baohuo as the legal tender, which was the first silver currency of legal count in Chinese currency history.

The silver *Ding* of *Cheng'an Baohuo* includes five levels which are 1 *Liang*, 1 *Liang* and a half, 2 *Liang* and a half, 5 *Liang* and 10 *Liang*. 1 *Liang* equaled to 2 *Guan*. The inscriptions on the silver *Ding* are: with *Cheng'an* written at the top, below which, the *Baohuo Yi Liang* (or *Baohuo Yi Liang Ban*) is on the right vertically, and the characters of *Ku* (storage) … *Bu* (department) … , *Ku*, *Bu* is on the left vertically, and with different signatures printed. So far, the existing silver *Ding* of *Cheng'an Baohuo* includes 1 *Liang* (approx. 40g) and 1 *Liang* and a half (approx. 60g), which are all in the shape of arched head and tightened up waist, with the silver percentage more than 95%. In 1200, as the copper and tin mixed silver *Ding* of the *Cheng'an Baohuo* was privately cast by the folks, it was banned at last.

> 元代钱币

元代是蒙古族于公元1206年建立的政权。元朝钱币以纸币为主，据实物推断，也铸有少量铜钱。元代禁止金银流通，但民间仍有使用白银的情形。并且，在元代确立了以白银为价值尺度的货币衡量制度。

铜钱

元代铜钱铸造量不多，在流通钱币中不占主要地位，主要有汉文钱、八思巴文钱、供养钱、权钞钱和农民起义军铸造的钱币。

汉文钱、八思巴文钱

汉文钱多为小平钱，折二、折三、折十，钱文有楷、篆书等，顺读或旋读。八思巴文钱钱文为八思巴文，反映出元钱中的本民族的色彩。

> Currencies of the Yuan Dynasty (1206-1368)

The authority of the Yuan Dynasty was established by the Mongolian in 1206. The currency of the Yuan Dynasty was mainly the paper money. According to the historical relic, there were several copper coins founded too. The circulation of the gold and silver were banned, however, there were still some silver currencies used by folks. And the government set a currency measurement system which used the silver as the meaure of value.

Copper Coins

The copper coin wasn't cast much in the Yuan Dynasty, which didn't take the main position among the circulating currencies. The main currencies included *Hanwen* money (coins inscribed with Chinese characters), *Basibawen* money

元世祖即位前，就铸有"大观通宝""大朝通宝""大朝合金"等钱；中统年间又铸"中统元宝"汉文楷、篆小平钱；至元二十二年（1285年）又铸"至元通宝"汉文钱、八思巴文钱。

元成宗元贞年间铸"元贞通宝"汉文钱、八思巴文钱，以及有"元贞元宝"汉文楷书折二钱；大德年间又铸"大德通宝"汉文钱、八思巴文钱。

元武宗至大年间铸"至大通宝""至大元宝"汉文钱，"大元通宝"汉文钱、八思巴文钱，"大元国宝"汉文钱等。

- 至大通宝（元）
Zhida Tongbao (Yuan Dynasty, 1206-1368)

(coins inscribed with Phagspa script), worship money, *Quanchao* money and the private moneys cast by the peasant insurrectionary armies.

Hanwen Money and *Basibawen* Money

Hanwen money was mainly *Xiaoping* money, *Zhe'er*, *Zhesan*, *Zheshi*, with the inscription of *Kai*, *Zhuan*, etc., which should be read in the regular or revolving orders. *Basibawen* money's inscription was written in the Phagspa script, which reveals the ethnic characteristic infiltrated in the currencies.

Before the reign of Emperor Shizu, the *Daguan Tongbao, Dachao Tongbao and Dachao Hejin* were cast. During the Zhongtong Period (1260-1263), the government cast the *Xiaoping* money of *Zhongtong Yuanbao* with the inscriptions of the fonts *Kai* and *Zhuan* written in Han language. In the 22nd year of the Zhiyuan Period (1285), the government cast the *Hanwen* money of *Zhiyuan Tongbao* and *Basibawen* money.

During the Yuanzhen Period (1295-1296), Emperor Chengzong cast the *Hanwen* money *Yuanzhen Tongbao* and *Basibawen* money, as well as *Yuanzhen Yuanbao* of *Zhe'er Qian* written in Han language of the font *Kai*. During the Dade

Period (1297-1307), the government cast the *Hanwen* money of *Dade Tongbao*, *Dayuan Tongbao*, *Dayuan Guobao*, *Basibawen* money, etc.

- 至大元宝（元）
  Zhida Yuanbao (Yuan Dynasty, 1206-1368)

- 大元国宝（元）
  Dayuan Guobao (Yuan Dynasty, 1206-1368)

- "大元通宝"八思巴文钱（元）
  Basibawen Money of *Dayuan Tongbao* (Yuan Dynasty, 1206-1368)

供养钱

供养钱是作为寺观供佛之用的钱币，由寺院自行铸造。元代的寺院属于官方统治的机构，上层僧侣是直接参政的官吏，因而供养钱实属官铸钱。虽然寺院拥有炉冶工场，但铸工技术远远比不上国家正规钱监，故所铸供养钱大多制作粗陋，钱形偏小，钱文拙劣，传世不多。元仁宗时，停铸行用钱，仅铸供养钱。天顺帝时大量铸造供养

Worship Money

Worship money as the currency used in the temples and monasteries was cast by the monasteries themselves. The monasteries belonged to the official ruling organization in the Yuan Dynasty. The upper monks were the government officials who could participate in political affairs. So the worship money actually was the official casted money. Though the temple owned the smelting workshop, yet the technique was no match for the

钱，到至元年间才始铸行用钱。

元代供养钱种类多样，按照钱面文字可分为：年号钱，如皇庆元宝、至治通宝、至顺之宝、大元至治等；寺院名称钱，如普庆寺、大帝觉寺、圣寿万安等；记年钱，如大德元年、至治元年等；佛家名号或记佛经钱，如宝珠菩萨、佛法僧宝等；进香钱，有进香直社等。供养钱上铸的图案多与道教、佛教相关，如八仙或"阿弥陀佛"等文字。

regular state-owned institution. So the most worship money were produced roughly and with relatively small size and clumsy inscriptions, which were rarely passed down. In the reign of Emperor Renzong, the government only cast the worship money instead of the circulating money. And so did Emperor Jinshun. In the Zhiyuan Period (1335-1340), the government started to cast circulating money.

The worship money of the Yuan Dynasty varied in many kinds. According to the facial inscription, it can be divided into: reign title money, like *Huangqing*

• 古钱币
Ancient Coins

权钞钱

权钞钱是顺帝至正年间所铸，是用来代表纸币的一种特殊钱币。权钞钱均铸造精整，钱体厚重，钱径大，钱文俊美，因铸造不多，行用不广，故传世罕见。其中，制作最为精美的当属"至正通宝"和"至正之宝"。

至正通宝：面背皆有内外郭，外郭宽平，内郭稍细，面文楷书，端庄秀丽，直读，有的钱背穿铸有八思巴文。

至正之宝：面文楷书，直读，钱背穿上铸"吉"字，表示铸造地为江西吉安，穿右铸"权钞"两字，穿左记值。面值有伍分、壹钱、壹钱伍分、贰钱伍分和伍钱五种。

• 至正之宝正面（元）
Front of *Zhizheng Zhibao* (Yuan Dynasty, 1206-1368)

Yuanbao, Zhizhi Tongbao, Zhishun Zhibao, Dayuan Zhizhi, etc.; temple money, like *Puqing* Temple, *Dadijue* Temple, *Shengshou Wan'an*, etc.; year money, like *Dade Yuannian, Zhizhi Yuannian*, etc.; Buddhist money or Sutras money, like *Baozhu Pusa, Fofa Sengbao*, etc.; pilgrim money, like *Jinxiang Zhishe*. The patterns of the worship money were mostly related to the Taoism and Buddhism, like the Eight Immortals or the characters *E Mi Tuo Fo* (Amitabha).

Quanchao Money

Quanchao money was a special money cast in the Zhizheng Period (1341-1367), which was used to represent the paper currency. *Quanchao* money was founded neatly, and with large diameter and thick, heavy body, and beautiful inscriptions. Due to the small foundry quantity and the narrow circulating extent, it was rarely seen in present days. Thereinto, the *Zhizheng Tongbao* and *Zhizheng Zhibao* were of the most beautiful production.

Zhizheng Tongbao: It has inner rim and outer rim at back. The outer rim is broad and flat; the inner rim is relatively thin. The facial inscription is written in *Kai* gracefully, which should be read vertically. Some of them have their back carved with Phagspa script.

• 至正之宝背面（元）
Back of the *Zhizheng Zhibao* (Yuan Dynasty, 1206-1368)

农民起义军钱币

元末农民起义军各自为政，大多铸行新钱。

元顺帝至正十三年（1353年），张士诚铸"天祐通宝"；至正十五年（1355年），韩林儿铸"龙凤通宝"；至正十八年（1358年），徐寿辉铸"天启通宝"；至正十九年（1359年），徐寿辉又铸"天定通宝"；至正二十年（1360年），陈

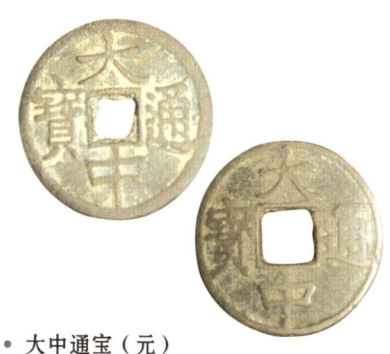

• 大中通宝（元）
Dazhong Tongbao (Yuan Dynasty, 1206-1368)

Zhizheng Zhibao: Its facial inscription is written in *Kai* which should be read vertically. It has the back carved with the character "吉" (*Ji*), representing the casting location, Ji'an of Jiangxi. The right part carved with the two characters *Quanchao*; while the left part carved with its value, including 5 Fen, 1 *Qian*, 1 *Qian* 5 *Fen*, 2 *Qian* 5 *Fen* and 5 *Qian*.

Peasant Insurrectionary Armies' Money

In the late Yuan Dynasty, the insurrectionary armies ruled their own manors separately. And most of them cast new currencies.

In the 13th year of the Zhizheng Period (1353), Zhang Shicheng cast *Tianyou Tongbao*; in 1355, Han Lin'er cast *Longfeng Tongbao*; in 1358, Xu Shouhui cast *Tianqi Tongbao*, in 1359, Xu Shouhui again cast *Tianding Tongbao*, in 1360, Chen Youliang cast *Dayi Tongbao*, in 1361, Zhu Yuanzhang cast *Dazhong Tongbao*.

These currencies were together called as "Warlords' currencies of the Late Yuan Dynasty", among which, the *Dazhong Tongbao* was commonly seen, while others were rare.

友谅铸"大义通宝";至正二十一年（1361年），朱元璋铸"大中通宝"。

这些钱合称为"元末群雄钱"，其中大中通宝钱常见，其余均少见。

纸币

纸币是元代的主要流通货币。元代实行银本位制度，以白银为价值尺度，发行的纸币有"交钞""银钞""中统交钞""中统元宝交钞""厘钞""至元通行宝钞""至大银钞""至正交钞"等。

元太宗八年（1236年）发行"交钞"，各地自行发行，互不流通，2—3年为一界；元宪宗三年（1253年）发行"银钞"，2—3年为一界，立银钞相权法，实行用钞统一与银比值，稳定币值，扩大纸币流通范围。

元世祖中统元年（1260年）发行"中统交钞"，以丝为本钱，以"两"为计量单位，二两当一两白银使用；接着，又发行"中统元宝交钞"，以"贯文"为计量单位，有十文、二十文、三十文、五十

Paper Money

Paper money was the main currency circulating in the Yuan Dynasty. The authority applied the silver standard system which used the silver as the measure of value. The issued paper moneys included *Jiaochao, Yinchao, Zhongtong Jiaochao, Zhongtong Yuanbao Jiaochao, Lichao, Zhiyuan Tongxing Baochao, Zhida Yinchao, Zhizheng Jiaochao*, etc.

In 1236, the local governments issued *Jiaochao* respectively. And the paper money could not be circulated among each other, with 2-3 years as one limit; in 1253, the government issued *Yinchao*, with 2-3 years as one limit, and set the *Yinchao Xiangquan* regulations, applied the unification of the currency, stabilized the silver exchange rate and expanded the circulation area.

In the 1st year of the Zhongtong Period (1260), Emperor Shizu of Yuan issued Zhongtong *Jiaochao*, with the silk as the standard, with *Liang* (2 *Liang* of the paper money equals to 1 *Liang* of the silver) as the unit. Successively, he issued the *Zhongtong Yuanbao Jiaochao*, with *Guan* and *Wen* as the unit, including 10 *Wen*, 20 *Wen*, 30 *Wen*, 50

文、一百文、二百文、三百文、五百文、一贯、二贯十个面值等级，一贯当一两中统交钞，二贯当一两银锭；至元十二年（1275年）又发行二文、三文、五文"厘钞"，作为辅币使用，三年后厘钞因使用不方便而废止；至元二十四年（1287年）又发行"至元通行宝钞"，与中统元宝交钞并行流通，在中统元宝交钞面值基础上增加五文面值，共十一个等级，一贯当五贯中统元宝交钞，二贯当一两银锭，二十贯当一两黄金。

Wen, 100 Wen, 200 Wen, 300 Wen, 500 Wen, 1 Guan, 2 Guan, totally ten value levels. 1 Guan of it equals to 1 Liang of Zhongtong Jiaochao; and 2 Guan of it equals to 1 Liang of silver ingot. In 1275, it issued Lichao with the values of 2 Wen, 3 Wen, and 5 Wen, as fractional currency. Three years later, due to its inconvenience, Lichao was banned. In the 24th year of the Zhiyuan Period (1287), the government issued Zhiyuan Tongbao Baochao, which was used with the Zhongtong Yuanbao Jiaochao at the same time. It added the nominal value of

- **中统元宝交钞五百文（元）**

  票面最上部从右到左是"中统元宝交钞"钞名，中部是面额、钱贯图案及"中统元宝"九叠篆文字样、"诸路通行"八思巴文字样，下部赏格印有发行单位、时间及赏格等内容。

  Zhongtong Yuanbao Baochao with the Value of 500 Wen (Yuan Dynasty, 1206-1368)

  At the top part of the money, from right to left, it's printed the money's name Zhongtong Yuanbao Jiaochao. In the middle, there are the nominal value, the patterns, the Zhongtong Yuanbao written in the font of Jiudie Zhuan, and the Zhulu Tongxing written in Phagspa script. At the bottom, it's printed the issue department, time, the reward, etc.

• 至元通行宝钞贰贯（元）

票面最上部从右到左印有"至元通行宝钞"钞名，其余形制与"中统元宝交钞"相似。

Zhiyuan Tongxing Baochao with the Value of 2 *Guan* (Yuan Dynasty, 1206-1368)

At the top part of the money, from right to left, it's printed the money's name *Zhiyuan Tongxing Baochao*. The rest parts are similar to the format of the *Zhongtong Yuanbao Jiaochao*.

元武宗至大二年（1309年）发行"至大银钞"，与中统元宝交钞、至元通行宝钞并行流通，面值从一厘到二两共分十三个等级，以"银两"为计值单位，一贯当二十五贯中统元宝交钞、五贯至元通行宝钞、一两白银、一钱黄金。由于严重贬值，财政恶化，仅发行了一年便废止；元顺帝至正十年（1350年）发行"至正交钞"，在

5 *Wen* on the basis of the ten value levels of *Zhongtong Yuanbao Jiaochao*, totally eleven levels. 1 *Guan* of it equals to 5 *Guan* of the *Zhongtong Yuanbao Jiaochao*; 2 *Guan* of it equals to 1 *Liang* silver ingot; 20 *Guan* equals to 1 *Liang* gold.

In the 2nd year of the Zhida Period (1309), Emperor Wuzong of Yuan issued *Zhida Yinchao*, which was circulated with the *Zhongtong Yuanbao Jiaochao*, *Zhiyuan Tongxing Baochao* at the same time. It has the nominal values ranging from 1 *Li* to 2 *Liang*, totally 13 levels, with the silver *Liang* as its unit. 1 *Guan* of it equals to 15 *Guan* of *Zhongtong Yuanbao Jiaochao*, 5 *Guan* of *Zhiyuan Tongxing Baochao*, 1 *Liang* of silver, 1 *Qian* of gold. Due to severe depreciation and the deterioration of the financial crisis, it was only issued for one year and then was banned. In the 10th year of the Zhizheng Period (1350), Emperor Shun of Yuan issued *Zhizheng Jiaochao*, which added the characters *Zhizheng Jiaochao* to the original format. 1 *Guan* of it equals to 2 *Guan* of *Zhongtong Jiaochao* and one thousand *Wen*.

Silver Ingot

The silver ingot of the Yuan Dynasty was also called as *Yuanbao*, which was cast by the government in 1266, with

原中统交钞上加印"至正交钞"字样，一贯当二贯中统交钞，合千文钱。

银锭

元代银锭又称"元宝"，由诸路宝钞都提举司在至元三年（1266年）用平淮库的白银铸造而成，以五十两为一锭。

元代元宝与南宋和金代的银锭形制相近，两端圆弧，当中束腰，呈马鞍形。所不同的是，元代元宝重量轻重不等，分为大、中、小铤。大铤重五十两，中铤重二十五两，小铤重十二两。正面錾刻地名、时间、重量、铸银官、银匠等；背面錾刻阴文"元宝"二字。

the silver from the Pinghuai Storage. 50 *Liang* of it equals to 1 *Ding*.

The shape of the Yuan's ingot is similar to the silver *Ding* of the Southern Song Dynasty and the Jin Dynasty (1115-1234), with round ends and tightened up waist, which is like a saddle. The difference between them is the weight. Yuan-dynasty ingots vary in different weights, including large, middle, and small *Ding*. The large *Ding* weighs 50 *Liang*; the middle one weighs 25 *Liang*; the small one weighs 12 *Liang*. The front side is carved with location name, time, weight, the casting governor, the craftsman, etc. The back side is carved two characters *Yuanbao* in intaglio.

- 真定路银锭（元）
Silver Ingot of Zhending (Yuan Dynasty, 1206-1368)

- 东平路宣课银锭（元）
Xuanke Silver Ingot of Dongping (Yuan Dynasty, 1206-1368)

> 明代钱币

1368年，朱元璋定都南京，年号洪武，建立明政权。明初大力推行纸币，实行以纸币为主，铜钱为辅，钱钞并用的货币制度。流通的钱大部分是唐宋旧钱，只有少数是本朝所铸。不久改为银钞两用，到明英宗时白银成为正式货币，以大小银锭元宝来流通。

铜钱

明代所铸铜钱为避太祖朱元璋名讳，钱文均用"通宝"，不用"元宝"，真书钱文，直读。

洪武元年（1368年），明太祖朱元璋始铸"洪武通宝"小平、折二、折三、折五、折十钱，钱文复杂，背面有素背、记值、记局之

> Currencies of the Ming Dynasty (1368-1644)

In 1368, Zhu Yuanzhang established the Ming Dynasty in Nanjing, with the reign title of Hongwu. In the early Ming Dynasty, the government promoted the paper money with great effort, and applied the coin-and-banknote currency system using the banknote as the main currency and copper coin as the auxiliary one. The circulated currencies mostly were the old ones of the Tang Dynasty and Song Dynasty; only rare ones were cast by the Ming Dynasty. Soon, the policy was changed into silver-and-banknote currency system. By the reign of Emperor Yingzong, silver became the official currency and was circulated in the forms of large or small silver ingots.

- 洪武通宝（明）
  Hongwu Tongbao (Ming Dynasty, 1368-1644)

- 洪武通宝背面（明）
  Back of *Hongwu Tongbao* (Ming Dynasty, 1368-1644)

- 永乐通宝（明）
  Yongle Tongbao (Ming Dynasty, 1368-1644)

- 嘉靖通宝（明）
  Jiajing Tongbao (Ming Dynasty, 1368-1644)

分；永乐六年（1408年）铸"永乐通宝"小平钱，主要作为对外贸易和赏赐之用；宣德八年至十年铸"宣德通宝"小平钱；弘治十六年至十八年铸"弘治通宝"小平钱；嘉靖七年（1528年）始铸"嘉靖通宝"小平钱；嘉靖十三年（1534年），仿洪武钱制，铸折二至折十记值大钱；隆庆四年（1570年）铸"隆庆通宝"小平钱；万历四年至四十八年铸"万历通宝"小平、折

Copper Coins

The copper coins cast in the Ming Dynasty were all called as *Tongbao instead of Yuanbao* to avoid the name taboo of Emperor Taizu, Zhu Yuanzhang. Its inscription was carved with the font *Zhen (Kai)* and was read vertically.

In the 1st year of the Hongwu Period (1368), Emperor Taizu, Zhu Yuanzhang firstly cast *Hongwu Tongbao*, with the value of *Xiaoping, Zhe'er, Zhesan, Zhewu, Zheshi*, and with complex

二钱；天启元年（1621年）铸"天启通宝"，并补铸年号钱"泰昌通宝"；崇祯元年至十七年铸"崇祯通宝"小平、折二、折五、折十钱。

明末农民起义军风起云涌，涌现出李自成和张献忠领导的两支农

- 隆庆通宝（明）
  Longqing Tongbao (Ming Dynasty, 1368-1644)

- 万历通宝（明）
  Wanli Tongbao (Ming Dynasty, 1368-1644)

inscriptions and different back patterns as plain back, value-marked, location-marked. In the 6th year of the Yongle Period (1408), the government cast *Xiaoping* coin Yongle Tongbao, which was mainly used in the foreign trade and awarding. During the time in the Xuande Period (1433-1435), the government cast *Xiaoping* coin *Xuande Tongbao*. During the time in the Hongzhi Period (1503-1505), the government cast *Xiaoping* coin *Hongzhi Tongbao*. In the 7th year of the Jiajing Period (1528), the government cast *Xiaoping* coin *Jiajing Tongbao*; In the 13th year of the Jiajing Period (1534), the government cast the value-marked large money with the nominal values ranging from *Zhe'er to Zheshi* by imitating the Hongwu Currency system. In the 4th year of the Longqing Period (1570), the government cast *Xiaoping* coin *Longqing Tongbao*. During the time in the Wanli Period (1576-1620), the government cast *Xiaoping* and *Zhe'er* coins of *Wanli Tongbao*. In the 1st year of the Tianqi Period (1621), the government cast *Tianqi Tongbao* and the reign title money *Taichang Tongbao*. During the time in the Chongzhen Period, the government cast *Chongzhen Tongbao* in *Xiaoping, Zhe'er, Zhewu, Zheshi*.

In the end of Ming Dynasty, the

• 天启通宝（明）
Tianqi Tongbao (Ming Dynasty, 1368-1644)

• 崇祯通宝（明）
Chongzhen Tongbao (Ming Dynasty, 1368-1644)

民起义军。这两支起义军分别建立了"大顺""大西"政权，并自铸钱币。

崇祯十七年（1644年），李自成铸"永昌通宝"小平、当五钱。

甲申年（1644年）冬，张献忠铸"大顺通宝"小平钱，制作精工，色泽金黄，背素或背穿下铸"户""工"等字。张献忠占据武昌称大西王时，铸"西王赏功"花钱，

• 永昌通宝（明）
Yongchang Tongbao (Ming Dynasty, 1368-1644)

peasant insurrectionary armies uprose throughout the nation, among which, the two main forces led by Li Zicheng and Zhang Xianzhong set up the Dashun and Daxi authorities respectively, and also cast their own currencies.

In 1644, Li Zicheng cast *Yongchang Tongbao* in *Xiaoping* and *Dangwu*.

In winter, Zhang Xianzhong cast *Dashun Tongbao* in *Xiaoping* coin, with fine production, golden color, and plain back or the back carved with the characters like *Hu* (户), *Gong* (工) below the string holes. When Zhang Xianzhong took Wuchang and granted himself the title of Daxi King, he cast the flower money of "Awarding Gold Coin of the West King" and gave them out to the soldiers who had battle achievements. It had three kinds as gold, silver, and copper, which was produced finely.

- 大顺通宝（明）
  Dashun Tongbao (Ming Dynasty, 1368-1644)

- 西王赏功金钱（明）
  Awarding Gold Coin of the West King (Ming Dynasty, 1368-1644)

奖赏给作战有功的将士。大顺通宝有金、银、铜三种，形制精致。

戊子年（1648年）张献忠义子孙可望自称东平王，铸造"兴朝通宝"小平、五厘、一分钱。小平钱背铸"工"字，五厘钱背铸"五厘"二字，一分钱背铸"壹分"二字。

In 1648, Zhang Xianzhong's adopted son, Sun Kewang granted himself the title of Dongping King, and cast *Xingchao Tongbao* in *Xiaoping*, *Wuli*, and *Yifen*. The *Xiaoping* coin had its back carved with the character *Gong*（工）; The *Wuli* coin had its back carved with *Wuli*（五厘）; The *Yifen* coin had its back carved with *Yifen*（壹分）.

南明钱币

南明是明亡后明的残余势力在南方建立的政权，包括弘光政权、隆武政权、鲁王监国、绍武政权及永历政权。其中，弘光政权、隆武政权、鲁王监国、永历政权四个政权曾铸有钱币。1644年，福王铸"弘光通宝"，鲁王铸"大明通宝"；1645年，唐王铸"隆武通宝"；1647年，桂王铸"永历通宝"。

Currencies of the Southern Ming Authorities

The Southern Ming authorities were established by the remaining forces of the original destroyed Ming Dynasty in the South, including the authorities of Hongguang, Longwu, Luwang Jianguo, Shaowu and Yongli, among which, the Hongguang authority, Longwu authority, Luwang Jianguo, Yongli authority once cast their own coins. In 1644, the King of Fu cast *Hongguang Tongbao*; and the King of Lu cast *Daming Tongbao*; In 1645, the King of Tang cast *Longwu Tongbao*; In 1647, the King of Gui cast *Yongli Tongbao*.

- 弘光通宝（南明）
  Hongguang Tongbao (Southern Ming Authority, 1644-1645)

- 永历通宝（南明）
  Yongli Tongbao (Southern Ming Authority, 1646-1662)

纸币

明代仅发行了一种纸币——明太祖洪武八年（1375年）发行的"大明通行宝钞"。据《明史·食货志》记载，大明通行宝钞以桑皮纸为原料，钞体呈竖长形，长一寸（约3.3厘米）、宽六寸（约20厘米），色泽泛青，外围为龙纹、缠枝莲花框，顶部横书钞名"大明通行宝钞"。内栏上端中部书写钞

Paper Money

There is only one kind of paper money in the Ming Dynasty, *Daming Tongxing Baochao* issued in the 8th year of the Hongwu Period (1375). According to the *Food and Money, History of Ming Dynasty*, *Daming Tongxing Baochao* used mulberry paper as the raw material. The body of the paper money is vertical rectangle, about 3.3 cm wide and 20 cm long. The background color is blue,

额,中部有钱贯图,两边分别书写"大明宝钞,天下通行"九叠篆文八字。下部赏格书写"户部奏准印造大明宝钞,与铜钱通行使用,伪造者斩,告捕者赏银贰佰伍拾两,仍给犯人财产。洪武年月日"。

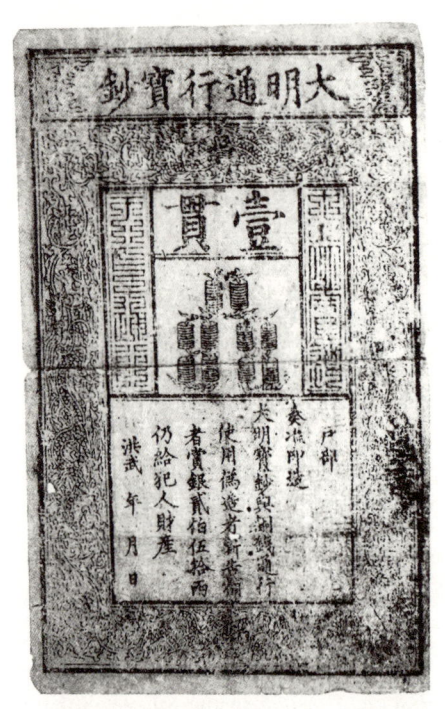

• **大明通行宝钞壹贯(明)**

大明宝钞图案雕刻细腻,文字简练。壹贯钞是大明通行宝钞中票幅最大的,也是迄今为止世界上票幅最大的纸币。

Daming Tongxing Baochao of one Guan (Ming Dynasty, 1368-1644)

Daming Baochao has delicate patterns and concise words. Its one–*Guan* bill was with the largest size of *Daming Tongxing Baochao*. It is also the largest paper money in the world until now.

with loong patterns and interlocking lotus borders and the name of the money *Daming Tongxing Baochao* written at the top horizontally. The denomination was written in the middle of the top part of the internal frame, the picture of the money string was in the middle part, and eight characters *Da Ming Bao Chao, Tian Xia Tong Xing* were written in *Jiudie Zhuanwen* on the right and left side of the frame respectively. In the bottom frame, there wrote "The Ministry of Revenue was allowed to print *Daming Baochao*. It is equivalent to copper coins. The forgers will be guillotined, but their properties will not be confiscated. Prosecutors will receive 250 *Liang* of silver which was expropriated from the convict. The Hongwu Period, Year, Month and Day."

All the *Daming Tongxing Baochao* used the reign title of Hongwu. *Baochao* is non-exchangeable money and only can be bought from the government by gold and silver. The nominal value contains six grades: 1 *Guan*, 500 *Wen*, 400 *Wen*, 300 *Wen*, 200 *Wen* and 100 *Wen*. 1 *Guan* of it equals to 1 *Liang* silver; 4 *Guan* of it equals to 1 *Liang* of gold. In the 22nd year of the Hongwu Period (1389), the government issued five kinds of money of small denominations: 10 *Wen*, 20 *Wen*,

大明通行宝钞均用洪武年号，属于不兑换纸币，只允许用金银向政府换购。面值有一贯、五百文、四百文、三百文、二百文、一百文六等，官价钱一贯当银一两、四贯当金一两。洪武二十二年（1389年），又增发小钞十文、二十文、三十文、四十文、五十文五种。后来，随着大明通行宝钞发行量的增大，逐渐贬值，发行不到二十年时间便趋于衰败。

银锭

明代中叶，银锭成为流通中的主要货币。明代银锭又称"马蹄银"，呈马蹄形，沿袭元代元宝形银锭形制，两端首部稍向外翘起，正面大于底部。

30 *Wen*, 40 *Wen* and 50 *Wen*. Shortly afterwards, *Daming Tongxing Baochao* depreciated due to the increasement of its issue quantity. It tended to decline after no more than 20 years.

Silver Ingot

In the mid-Ming Dynasty, the silver ingot became the main circulating currency. According to its appearance, it was also called as "horseshoe silver", which followed the *Yuanbao* shape of the Yuan Dynasty, with two ends perking outwards and bigger front than the bottom.

The silver ingot of the Ming Dynasty was mearsured by *Liang*, and had four forms, including large, middle, small, fraction. The large one was shaped as a boat, weighing about 50 *Liang*, being carved with casting location, weight,

- 正德八年银锭（明）
Silver Ingot of the 8th Year of the Zhengde Period (Ming Dynasty, 1368-1644)

- 金花银银锭（明）
Silver Ingot of Gold Flower Silver (Ming Dynasty, 1368-1644)

明代银锭以"两"为计量单位，有大、中、小、碎银四种形制。大锭呈船形，重约五十两，錾刻铸造地、重量和银匠姓名等铭文，用于完粮纳赋和大宗交易。有些大银锭有重近百斤、五百两、一百两者，都是非常规铸造的大锭。中锭、小锭和碎银，形制较为复杂，铭文字数不一。有些小银锭，上面只錾刻年号。碎银重量多在一两以下，主要用于小额支付或找零。

明代初期银锭的铭文多是阴文，也兼用阳文。明代中叶前后，铭文多是阳文。

the name of the craftsman, etc., which was used in the taxation and block trade. Some of the large ingots weighed almost 50 kg, 500 *Liang* (25 kg), 100 *Liang* (5 kg), which were founded unconventionally. The middle, small and fraction ones were with complex shapes and forms, as well as different inscription characters. Some small ingots only were carved with the reign title. The fraction ingot mainly weighed no more than 50 g, and was mostly used to pay for the small check or give change.

In the early stage of the Ming Dynasty, the inscription of the silver ingot was mostly carved in intaglio, sometimes in relief. In the middle and late period, the inscription was mainly in relief.

- 嘉靖甲辰银锭（明）
Silver Ingot of the Jiajing Period (Ming Dynasty, 1368-1644)

银锭的形制

银锭有船形、条形和饼形三种形状。一般船形的银锭称为银锭，条形的银锭称为银铤，饼形的银锭称为银饼。

Shapes of Silver Ingot

The silver ingot was produced in three shapes, including boat-shaped, bar-shaped, and cake-shaped. The boat-shaped one was called as silver ingot; The bar-shaped one was called as silver *Ding*; The cake-shaped was called as silver plate.

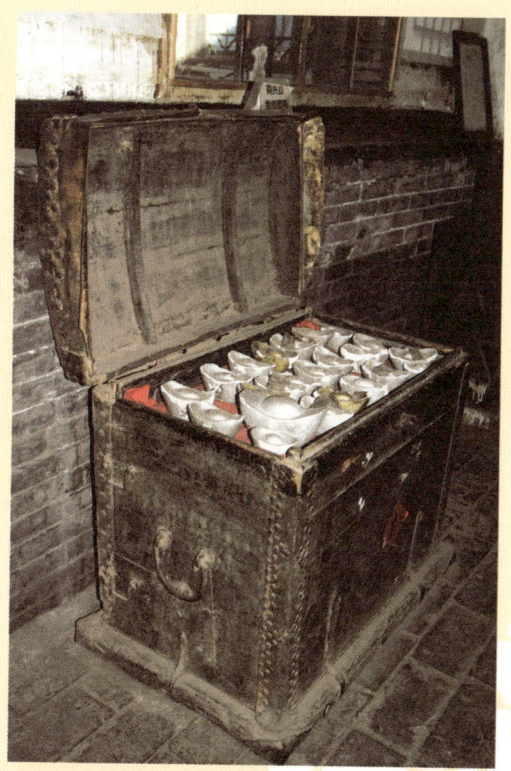

- 银锭
Silver Ingot

> 清代钱币

清朝是中国古代最后一个封建王朝，其货币制度承袭明朝的银钱并用制，而白银的地位更加重要。清末，中国在外国资本主义的强力冲击下，通用了两千多年的方孔圆钱走向衰落，逐步被纸币、机制铜元、机制银元代替。清政府还建立了银行，发行兑换券。外国列强乘势而入，相继在中国设立银行，发行货币，掠夺中国财产。

铜钱

清代方孔圆钱采用传统的翻砂铸造工艺，在继承前朝的风格上有所进步。钱体更显扁小，边郭宽阔，钱文均以年号连通宝，书体前期普遍采用宋体，咸丰、同治后逐步以楷体、宋体兼行。由于从顺治以后各省设局分散铸币，因此清代铜钱铸量大，种类繁多。

> Currencies of the Qing Dynasty (1616-1911)

As the last feudal dynasty in ancient China, Qing Dynasty inherited the coinage system from the previous Ming Dynasty with silver ingot playing a more significant role. Under fierce impact of foreign capitalism, the circular coin (with a square hole), which used to be the currency in vogue for over two thousand years, was on the wane and gradually replaced by paper currency, machine-made copper and silver coins during the final stages of imperial China. Moreover, banks were established by the Qing government to issue coin certificate. Availing themselves of the opportunity, foreign powers set up banks in succession in China, plundering wealth by currency issuing.

Copper Coins

The circular coins (with a square hole) issued in the Qing Dynasty were cast

天命汗钱、天命通宝、天聪汗钱

清在入关之前，清太祖努尔哈赤天命元年（1616年）铸"天命汗钱"满文钱，"天命通宝"汉文、满文钱。清太宗皇太极天聪元年（1627年）铸"天聪汗钱"满文钱。

- **天聪汗钱（清）**
天聪汗钱为满文折十钱，钱文左上右下读。
Tiancong Hanqian (Qing Dynasty, 1616-1911)
The *Tiancong Hanqian* was inscribed by Man language with the nominal value of *Shiqian*, and was read from the upper left to the bottom right.

顺治通宝

清兵入关后，清世祖顺治元年（1644年）在京师设户部宝泉局和工部宝源局，铸造"顺治通宝"。顺治通宝版式较多，可归纳为五类，俗称"顺治五式"：仿明式

in moulds made from a mixture of sand and clay (sand-copy-casting method). Compared with the coins cast in the pervious dynasties, they are featured with a better style, for they are smaller and thinner and have wider rims. The inscriptions are all carved with the reign title and the words *Tongbao*. The font of *Song* was widely used in the early stage and was later gradually joined by the regular script (*Kai*) after the Xianfeng and Shunzhi periods. After the Shunzhi Period, each province began to have its own establishment for coinage casting, which resulted in the large number and variety of Qing Dynasty copper coins.

Tianming Hanqian, Tianming Tongbao, Tiancong Hanqian

Emperor Taizu, Nurhaci ordered to cast *Tianming Hanqian* of Man language, *Tianming Tongbao* of Han and Man languages in the 1st year of the Tianming Period (1616). In the 1st year of the Tiancong Period (1627), Emperor Taizong, Huang Taiji ordered to cast *Tiancong Hanqian* of Man language.

Shunzhi Tongbao

In the 1st year of the Shunzhi Period (1644), Emperor Shizu established *Baoquan Ju* under the Hu Department (the Ministry of Revenue in feudal China) and

• "顺治通宝"仿明式钱（清）
Ming-Style *Shunzhi Tongbao* (Qing Dynasty, 1616-1911)

• "顺治通宝"背一厘钱背面（清）
Back of the *Yili* Money of *Shunzhi Tongbao* (Qing Dynasty, 1616-1911)

• "顺治通宝"背满汉文记局钱（清）
背文右为汉字局名"原"，左为满文。
Bureau-marked Money of Man and Han Languages of *Shunzhi Tongbao* (Qing Dynasty, 1616-1911)

The back inscription on the right is the bureau name of *Yuan* in Han language; the one on the left is written in Man language.

Baoyuan Ju under the *Gong* Department (the Ministry of Works in feudal China) to cast *Shunzhi Tongbao*. *Shunzhi Tongbao* varied in many versions which could be concluded into five categories called "Five Categories of Shunzi": Ming-style money, was cast during 1644-1646, with inscription of *Kai*, plain back, seldom having patterns of stars, the moon, and the sun; bureau-marked money of Han language, was cast in 1644, imitating the *Kaiyuan* money of Huichang in Tang Dynasty, with the bureau name inscribed on its back; *Yili* money, was cast in 1653, which was *Zheyin* money. 1 *Wen* of it equaled to 1 *Li* silver. It was with two characters "*Yili*" carved on the left side of the back and the bureau name carved on the right side; bureau-marked money of Man language, was cast in 1660, with facial inscription of Han language, and the bureau names of *Baoquan* or *Baoyuan* written in Man language carved on the left and right side of its back respectively; bureau-marke money of Man and Han languages, was cast in 1660, with facial inscription of Han language, and the bureau names written in Man language and Han language carved on the left and right sides of its back respectively.

Kangxi Tongbao

钱，顺治元年至三年铸，钱文楷书，多光背，少有星纹、月纹、日纹；背汉文记局钱，顺治元年（1644年）铸，仿唐会昌开元钱式，背文记局；背一厘钱，顺治十年（1653年）铸，是折银钱，每文值银一厘，背穿左有"一厘"二字，穿右为局名；背满文记局钱，顺治十七年（1660年）铸，面文汉文，背穿左右为"宝泉"或"宝源"满文局名；背满汉文记局钱，顺治十七年（1660年）铸，面文汉文，背文穿左为满文局名，穿右为汉字局名。

康熙通宝

康熙元年（1662年），铸"康熙通宝"，铸造精美，钱型厚重，铸量极大，存世很多，分为背满文记局钱和背满汉文记局钱两种。背满文记局钱为宝泉、宝源两局所铸，背满文记局。背满汉文记局钱穿左满文，穿右汉文记局。

In the 1st year of the Kangxi Period (1662), *Kangxi Tongbao* was cast, which had beautiful appearance, with thick and heavy shape and was cast in large quantity. A lot of them have been saved till today. They are divided into two categories according to the back inscriptions of the money which records its producing bureau. One category is the money using the Man language as the back inscription of the bureau and the other one is the money using the Man and the Han languages as the back inscription of the bureau. The money using the Man language as the back text of the bureau is cast by *Baoquan* and *Baoyuan* bureaus. On the money using the Man and the Han languages as the back inscription of the bureau, the left of it is the Man language and the right of it is the Han language.

- 康熙通宝（清）
  Kangxi Tongbao (Qing Dynasty, 1616-1911)

罗汉钱

罗汉钱是康熙年间宝泉局铸造的一种特殊的"康熙通宝"钱，罗汉钱最早叫"万寿钱"，是为庆祝康熙皇帝60岁生日，户部一局特制的一种铜钱。其形制与普通的"康熙通宝"小平钱差不多，只是面文笔画略有变化。罗汉钱制作精美，色泽金黄，深受人们喜爱。

- 罗汉钱（清）
Arhat Coin (Qing Dynasty, 1616-1911)

Arhat Coin

Arhat coin was a special currency from *Baoquan Ju* during the Kangxi Period in the Qing Dynasty. Originally called "long life" coin, it was specially made by The Ministry of Revenue No.1 Bureau to celebrate Emperor Kangxi's 60th birthday. It shared the similar shape with common *Xiaoping* coin during the Period of Kangxi except the slight stroke difference on its side. Delicately-made arhat coin with golden yellow color was quite popular among people.

雍正通宝、乾隆通宝、嘉庆通宝、道光通宝

雍正元年（1723年）铸"雍正通宝"，背有二满文，左为宝字，右为各省局名。

乾隆元年（1736年）铸"乾隆通宝"，初铸称黄钱（未加锡），后铸称青钱（加锡），背满文记

Yongzheng Tongbao, Qianlong Tongbao, Jiaqing Tongbao, Daoguang Tongbao

The *Yongzheng Tongbao* was cast in the 1st year of the Yongzheng Period (1723). At the back of it there are two words in the language of Man. The left is the name of the coin and the right are names of the authorities in every province.

The *Qianlong Tongbao* was cast

- 雍正通宝雕母（清）
Carved Mother Model of *Yongzheng Tongbao* (Qing Dynasty, 1616-1911)

- 雍正通宝雕母背面（清）
Back of Carved Mother Model of *Yongzheng Tongbao* (Qing Dynasty, 1616-1911)

- 乾隆通宝雕母（清）
Carved Mother Model of *Qianlong Tongbao* (Qing Dynasty, 1616-1911)

局。乾隆二十四年（1759年），清统一了新疆，新疆流通原来的红铜无孔"普尔"钱，也称"新疆红钱"，在喀什、叶尔羌、库车等地区以一当十，在其他地区则以一当一。

嘉庆元年（1796年）铸"嘉庆通宝"，背铸星月纹，满文记局。

道光元年（1821年）铸"道光通宝"，背满文记局，在嘉庆通宝基础上增加库车、宝新两个钱局。

in the 1st year of the Qianlong Period (1736). At first, it was called the yellow money (without nickel) and later was called the green money (with nickel added), at the back of which are the names of authorities in the language of Man. In the 24th year of the Qianlong Period (1759), Qing government unified Xinjiang. The previous copper coin Pu'er without a hole, which was also called "Xinjiang red coin", equaled to ten

• 嘉庆通宝雕母（清）
Carved Mother Model of the *Jiaqing Tongbao* (Qing Dynasty, 1616-1911)

• 道光通宝雕母（清）
Carved Mother Model of *Daoguang Tongbao* (Qing Dynasty, 1616-1911)

Qianlong Tongbao in Kashgar, Yarkant and Kuqa but in other areas equaled to one *Qianlong Tongbao*.

The *Jiaqing Tongbao* was cast in the 1st year of the Jiaqing Period (1796). There are patterns of stars and moon at the back of the coin, with names of the authorities carved in Man language.

The *Daoguang Tongbao* was cast in the 1st year of the Daoguang Period (1821), at the back of which are names of authorities in Man language. On the basis of *Jiaqing Tongbao*, two money bureaus, Kuqa and *Baoxin*, were added.

三藩钱

清政府封明朝将领吴三桂为平西王镇守云南，封耿仲明为靖南王镇守福建，封尚可喜为平南王镇守广东，史称"三藩"。他们铸造的"利用通宝""昭武通宝""裕民通宝""洪化通宝"称为"三藩钱"。其中平南王尚可喜在清军的猛攻下，很快归降，没有铸钱。

利用通宝：吴三桂镇守滇南时所铸，背文有记地名、记值，仅在当地通行。

昭武通宝：康熙十二年（1673年）吴三桂称帝后所铸，钱文真、篆二体，书体优美。

裕民通宝：康熙十三年（1674年）耿仲明之孙耿精忠所铸。

洪化通宝：康熙十八年（1679年）吴三桂之孙吴世所铸，背文有"户""工"字样。

Moneys of Three Military Governors

The government of the Qing Dynasty offered the Ming General Wu Sangui the title of "Governor of Pingxi", guarding Yunnan. Geng Zhongming was offered the title of "Governor of Jingnan", guarding Fujian. And Shang Kexi was appointed the title of "Governor of Pingnan", guarding Guangdong. The three were called "the Three Military Governors" in history. The money they made which were called *Liyong Tongbao*, *Zhaowu Tongbao*, *Yumin Tongbao* and *Honghua Tongbao* known as "Moneys of Three Military Governors". While the governor of Pingxi, Shang Kexi, didn't cast coins under the fierce onslaught of the troops of Qing and quickly surrendered.

Liyong Tongbao: It was made when Wu Sangui was guarding the south of Yunnan. There were the place names and note values at the back of the coin. The coin was only circulated in the local area.

Zhaowu Tongbao: It was made in 1673 after Wu Sangui granted himself as the emperor. The inscriptions were written in two fonts of Zhen and Zhuan gracefully.

Yumin Tongbao: It was made by Geng Jingzhong, the grandson of Geng Zhongming in 1674.

Honghua Tongbao: It was made by Wu Shi who was the grandson of Wu Sangui in 1679. There were Chinese characters of *Hu* (户) and *Gong* (工) on the back the coin.

- 利用通宝背面（清）

  Back of *Liyong Tongbao* (Qing Dynasty, 1616-1911)

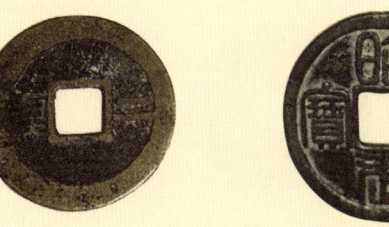

- 昭武通宝（清）

  Zhaowu Tongbao (Qing Dynasty, 1616-1911)

- 洪化通宝（清）

  Honghua Tongbao (Qing Dynasty, 1616-1911)

咸丰、同治、光绪、宣统铜钱

咸丰元年（1851年）铸"咸丰通宝""咸丰重宝""咸丰元宝"；咸丰十一年（1861年）铸"祺祥通宝""祺祥重宝"，仅行用了69天，便被废除，是中国使用时间最短的钱币。同治元年（1862年）铸"同治通宝""同治重宝"。光绪元年（1875年）铸"光绪通宝""光绪重宝"，铸造精美，钱文楷书，端庄秀丽。宣统元年（1909年）铸"宣统通宝"，铸量很小。

Copper Coins of the Periods of Xianfeng, Tongzhi, Guangxu, and Xuantong

Xianfeng Tongbao, *Xianfeng Zhongbao*, and *Xianfeng Yuanbao* were manufactured in the 1st year of the Xianfeng Period (1851). *Qixiang Tongbao* and *Qixiang Zhongbao* were manufactured in the 11th year of the Xianfeng Period (1861), and had the shortest currency time because they were abolished 69 days after they were issued. *Tongzhi Tongbao* and *Tongzhi Zhongbao* were manufactured in the 1st year of the Tongzhi Period (1862). *Guangxu Tongbao* and *Guangxu Zhongbao* were manufactured in the 1st year of the Guangxu Period (1875) and were delicately founded. The inscriptions were in regular scripts (*Kai*), dignified and beautiful. *Xuantong Tongbao* was manufactured in the 1st year of the Xuantong Period (1909) with a small amount.

- 咸丰通宝雕母（清）
Carved Mother Model of *Xianfeng Tongbao* (Qing Dynasty, 1616-1911)

- 咸丰重宝雕母（清）
Carved Mother Model of *Xianfeng Zhongbao* (Qing Dynasty, 1616-1911)

- 祺祥通宝（清）
Qixiang Tongbao (Qing Dynasty, 1616-1911)

- 同治通宝（清）
  Tongzhi Tongbao (Qing Dynasty, 1616-1911)

- 宣统通宝（清）
  Xuantong Tongbao (Qing Dynasty, 1616-1911)

太平天国及其他起义军铜钱

清咸丰初年，洪秀全聚众起事于广西桂平金田村，建号太平天国。1853年3月，洪秀全攻占南京，建立太平天国政权。太平天国农民政权（1851—1864）铸有"太平天国""平靖胜宝"。钱文和制作不统一，钱的等级各地也不一致。太平天国有小平、折二、折三、折五、当十等多种。平靖胜宝为花钱，背文为军营名称。

上海小刀会起义军（1853—1855）铸"太平通宝"，背铸日月纹，表达反清复明之意。

Copper Coins of Taiping Heavely Kingdom (1851-1864) and Other Insurgent Groups

In the early Xianfeng Period, Qing Dynasty, Hong Xiuquan led an uprising in Jintian Village of Guiping County, Guangxi, claiming to be the Taiping Heavenly Kingdom. In March, 1853, Hong Xiuquan occupied Nanjing and then established Taiping Heavenly Kingdom regime. *Taiping Tianguo* and *Pingjing Shengbao* were two kinds of coins made by this peasant authority. The characters and making methods were not consistent, neither was the rank of these coins in different areas. There were more than ten kinds of coins including *Xiaoping, Zhe'er, Zhesan, Zhewu, Dangshi*, etc. *Pingjing Shengbao* was a kind of flower money with names of military camps carved on their backs.

Shanghai Small Swords Society (1853-1855) made *Taiping Tongbao* with the sun-and-moon design cast on their backs, expressing their determination of opposing the Qing and restoring the Ming.

- 太平天国（清）
  Taiping Tianguo (Qing Dynasty, 1616-1911)

铜元

铜元，清末开始使用的各种新式铜质辅币的通称。与传统的铜钱不同，圆形，中间无孔，俗称铜板。铜元出现后，很快就取代方孔圆钱，成为主要货币。

光绪元宝

光绪二十三年（1897年），经西道监察御史陈其璋奏请仿造大小铜元，补制钱的不足。光绪二十六年（1900年），"光绪元宝"铜元在广东试铸成功。

光绪元宝正面为"光绪元宝"四字汉文和"广宝"二字满文，上缘为制造铜元的省份名称或制造局名，下缘为面值，周围有"每百枚换一圆"的字样。背面中央刻有各种各样、变化多端的蟠龙纹饰，上

- 光绪元宝（清）
  Guangxu Yuanbao (Qing Dynasty, 1616-1911)

Copper Coins

Copper coin, was the general name of various new copper fractional money used in the late Qing Dynasy. Different from traditional copper coin, it is of circle form, without a hole in the middle, and is generally called *Tongban* (coin made of copper). Since the copper coin appeared, it soon took place of the circular coin (with a square hole), and become the main currency in China.

Guangxu Yuanbao

In the 23rd year of the Guangxu Period (1897), Chen qizhang, the Investigating Censor of Western Circuits, submitted a memorial to the emperor and suggested to counterfeit copper coins in case to make up the tight circulation of money. In the 26th year of the Guangxu Period (1900), the *Guangxu Yuanbao* copper coin was cast successfully in Guangdong.

There were four Chinese characters *Guang*, *Xu*, *Yuan* and *Bao* on the obverse side and two Man characters *Guang Bao* on the reverse side. The name of cast bureau or province was cast on the upper rim of the obverse, and the value on the lower rim. Moreover, the writing of "100 coins' value is equal to 1 silver Yuan" appeared on the circumference. The

下缘用英文标明制造省份或制造局名和面值等。每枚重二钱，除广东所造有少数对银作价外，其余都是对制钱作价，主要有一文、二文、五文、十文和二十文、三十文等面值。当制钱十文，每百枚换银元一元，版别复杂。

大清铜币

光绪三十一年（1905年），清政府整顿币制，限制各省铜元铸额，令天津户部造币总厂制造"大清铜币"，并确定"大清铜币"为法定货币，户部将新币祖模颁发给各省，仿效制造。

大清铜币正面中部为"大清铜币"四字汉文，在四字币文的中心添加地名简称，上端是"大清铜币"四字满文，满文的两侧是干支

- 大清铜币（清）
  Copper Coin of the Qing Dynasty (Qing Dynasty, 1616-1911)

various loong patterns was decorated in the cetral of reverse side, and in the upper and lower they were the English writing of the name of bureau or province where it was cast . Per coin weights two *Qian* (1 *Qian* equals to 5 g). The value of coin was set offically except some of Guangdong Province, where they set the value of the silver. They included six common values, 1 *Wen*, 2 *Wen*, 5 *Wen*, 10 *Wen*, 20 *Wen* and 30 *Wen*. Each copper coin values 10 *Wen*, and 100 copper coins are equal to 1 silver Yuan. The versions of the copper coin are various.

Copper Coin of the Qing Dynasty

In the 31st year of the Guangxu Period (1905), the Qing government reframed the copper currency system by putting restrictions on the quantity of copper coins cast by provincial governments and mandating the Tianjin General Mint of Ministry of Revenue to design the Copper Coin of the Qing Dynasty, which was then defined as the legal tender by law. The provincial governments then cast coins accordingly with the coin ancestor model provided by The Ministry of Revenue (*Hu* Department).

The head of Copper Coin of the Qing Dynasty was inscribed with an abbreviation of the production place in the

记年，左右两旁为"户部"二字，后改为"度支部"三字，下端标明面值，背面中部为蟠龙图纹，上端是"光绪年造"或"宣统年造"，下端是英文"大清帝国铜币"。面额为一文、二文、五文、十文、二十文、三十文。

银两

清代银两制度有了很大发展，多以马蹄形的元宝出现，也称为"宝银"。银两经过熔铸，分为中锭、小锭、碎银、滴珠等。元宝重约五十两（2.5千克），中锭重约十两，大多呈秤锤状，又称"银锞子"，小锭三两至五两不等，形如馒头，又叫"小锞银"；碎银、滴珠等则都是一两以下的银屑。清代银两作为称量货币，使用很不方便。而且银两繁琐庞杂，各地均使用不同成色名目的银两，相互兑换还要按一定的比率折算。

鸦片战争后，外国银元大量流入，自铸银元流行，都没有根本改变或取代银两制度的地位。1933年，废两改元后银两才不再使用。

center, four Chinese characters, "大清铜币" (Copper Coin of the Qing Dynasty), circling around the center character, the Man expression of the year designated by Heavenly Stems and Earthly Branches on the top, two Chinese characters, "户部" (Ministry of Revenue), which was replaced by "度支部" (Ministry of Treasury) in later versions, on the left and right respectively, and the nominal value of the coin on the bottom. 4 characters of Man language in the middle were issued in 6 denominations: 1 *Wen*, 2 *Wen*, 5 *Wen*, 10 *Wen*, 20 *Wen*, and 30 *Wen*. The tail of the coin is cast with the coiling loong pattern in the middle, four Chinese characters, "光绪年造" or "宣统年造" (the year of the Guangxu Period or Xuantong Period) on the top, as well as the English words "Tai Ching Ti Kuo Copper Coin" on the bottom.

Silver Ingot

The currency system of the Qing Dynasty had developed a lot. The main currency was the horseshoe-shaped *Yuanbao*, also called as *Baoyin*. The silver was melted and divided into middle ingot, small ingot, fraction silver, drop beads, etc. *Yuanbao* weighs about 50 *Liang* (2.5 kg); the middle ingot weighs about 10 *Liang*

• 咸丰八年太谷县元宝锭（清）
Yuanbao Ingot of Taigu County of the 8th Year of the Xianfeng Period (Qing Dynasty, 1616-1911)

• 道光八年新昌县方锭（清）
Square Ingot of Xinchang County of the 8th Year of the Daoguang Period (Qing Dynasty, 1616-1911)

银元

由于外国银元的大量流入，中国足色纹银大量外流，于是清政府开始自制机制银元。银元没有统一的标准，各地银元的图案、文字、重量和成色差异较大，但背面都铸有龙的图案，因此，清代银元也被称作"龙洋"。光绪十年（1884

(0.5 kg), mostly was shaped in hammer-shaped weight, also calle as *Yinkezi*; the small ingot weighs 3-5 *Liang* (0.15-0.25 kg), with the shape like the steamed bread, also called as *Xiaokeyin*; fraction silver and drop beads are of the weight less than 1 *Liang* (50 g). The silver currencies used in the Qing Dynasty were not convenient for exchange, and with extremely complex kinds which varied in percentage and names in different areas. It should be converted according to a certain ratio while being used.

After the Opium War, although the foreign silver coins inflowed and the privately cast silver coins were prevailed, the currency system of silver ingot didn't replaced until 1933, the government announced to ban the silver ingot and change to silver coin.

Silver Coins

Due to the great inflow of the foreign silver coins, Chinese fine silver of standard purity flew out in a large scale. So the government started to produce the machine-cast silver coins. The silver coin doesn't have a unified standard, which varies in pattern, character, weight and purity percentage in different areas. However, all of them have their back

年），吉林机器局铸造出了中国第一套机制银币"吉林厂平银币"，有一两、七钱、五钱、三钱、一钱五种币值，开创了中国机制币的先河。清代银元主要有"光绪元宝""宣统元宝"和"大清银币"。

光绪元宝

清光绪十五年（1889年），张之洞在广东率先制造"光绪元宝"银元，各省纷纷效仿。因大量流入中国的外国银元重量轻于七钱三分，所以，七钱三分"光绪元宝"银元逐渐将外国银元驱逐出境。光绪十六年（1890年），"光绪元宝"银元改铸为七钱二分，作为法定货币，广泛流通。"光绪元宝"银元有大小五等，版别较复杂，正面中部为币名，上缘标注制造银元

- "光绪元宝"银元（清）
Silver Coin of *Guangxu Yuanbao* (Qing Dynasty, 1616-1911)

carved with the pattern of loong. So the silver coin of the Qing Dynasty was also called as "Loong Coin". In 1884, The Jilin Machinery Company cast the first set of machine-made silver coin "Jilin Changping Silver Coin", with the value of 1 *Liang*, 7 *Qian*, 5 *Qian*, 3 *Qian*, and 1 *Qian*, which initiated the machine-made coins' foundry in China. The silver coins are mainly *Guangxu Yuanbao*, *Xuantong Yuanbao* and *Daqing Yinbi*.

Guangxu Yuanbao

In 1889, Zhang Zhidong firstly cast *Guangxu Yuanbao* silver coin in Guangdong Province, which was followed by other provinces successively. As the foreign silver coin was lighter than 7 *Qian* 3 *Fen*, so the *Guangxu Yuanbao* with the weight of 7 *Qian* 3 *Fen* gradually expelled the foreign coins out of China. In 1890, *Guangxu Yuanbao* was changed into 7 *Qian* 2 *Fen*, and was circulated widely as the legal tender. *Guangxu Yuanbao* silver coin has five grades in size and is with complex versions. It is with the coin name in the middle, and the casting provinces' name or the companies' name marked above, and the nominal value printed below. It has its back carved with the pattern of loong in the center and the province name

中国最早的人像币

光绪三十二年（1906年），四川成都造币厂铸造的四川卢比银币，正面用光绪皇帝的半身侧面像，是中国货币史上最早出现的人像币，也是唯一铸有中国帝王的货币。四川卢比银币仿印度卢比式样，背铸"四川省造"四字，环绕花草纹饰，有竖花、横花两种版别。面值分为一元、半元和四分之一元三种规格。

The Earliest Portrait Coins in China

In 1906, Sichuan silver rupee coins were made in Chengdu Mint, Sichuan Province. With a bust of Emperor Guangxu on the right side, they were the earliest potrait coin in the history of Chinese currency, as well as the only currency with the portrait of Chinese Emperors. They imitated the pattern of the Indian rupee coins, with the Chinese character "四川省造 (Made in Sichuan Province)" in the back of the coins surrounded by flowers and grasses as the decoration. There are two kinds of versions as vertical flowers and horizontal owers. The denomination of the coins could be divided into three kinds, as 1 Yuan, half Yuan and a quarter Yuan.

- **四川卢比银币（清）**
  四川卢比银币仿印度卢比式样制成，故名。
  Sichuan Rupee Coin (Qing Dynasty, 1616-1911)
  As it was made by imitating the style of the Indian rupee coin, so it was called Sichuan rupee coin.

的省份名称，或制造局名，下缘标明币值；背面中部为蟠龙图案，上缘和下缘分别用英文注明省份名称和币值。此外，也有少数不符合此种格式的银元，图案格式差异较大。

宣统元宝

宣统年间制造，形制和"光绪元宝"银元相同，以"元"为单位，面值有一元、五角、二角、一角、五分五种。各省根据自己的需要，

and nominal value printed in Engilsh in the upper and bottom part respectively. Besides, there were seldom silver coins which didn't fit the standards and with great differences in pattern and format.

Xuantong Yuanbao

The *Xuantong Yuanbao* was made during the Xuantong Period (1909-1911). It was shaped as the silver coin of *Guangxu Yuanbao*, with Yuan as the unit. There were five kinds of denominations: 1

• 光绪三十年大清银币（清）
Silver Coin of the 30th Year of the Guangxu Period (Qing Dynasty, 1616-1911)

• 宣统三年大清银币（清）
Silver Coin of the 3rd Year of the Xuantong Period (Qing Dynasty, 1616-1911)

因地制造。

宣统三年（1911年）新疆喀什地区还制造出面值为五钱的"宣统元宝"银元，富有浓厚的民族色彩。

大清银币

光绪三十年（1904年），湖北省率先制造"一两"大清银币，其后少数省份也跟进制造，由于流通

Yuan, 5 Jiao, 2 Jiao, 1 Jiao, and 5 Fen. Every province made the silver coin on its own, according to its needs.

In the 3rd year of the Xuantong Period (1911), *Xuantong Yuanbao* of the value of 5 *Qian* was manufactured in Kashgar area, Xinjiang, which was characterized by strong ethnic style.

Silver Coin of Qing Dynasty

Hubei Province was the first to produce Silver Coin of the Qing Dynasty in 1904, which was in denomination of 1 *Liang*. Then, a few more provinces followed suit. The production was forced to stop as a result of poor circulation while some other provinces turned to produce Silver Coin of Qing Dynasty in denomination of 1 *Yuan*. Versions of coins varied in different provinces. In 1910, the Ministry of Treasury of the Qing Government promulgated with imperial permit the Currency Regulations, setting "*Yuan*" as the standard monetary unit and silver coins as national currency, eliminating the silver system, banning production of silver coin by provinces, reverting the casting rights to the central government and issuing strict rules on the weight and fineness of silver coins. In the same year, headquarters of the coinage factories in Tianjin produced a new trial version of

不畅，被迫停止制造，有的则改制"壹圆"大清银币。制造省份不同，版别迥异。宣统二年（1910年），清政府度支部奏准颁布《币制则例》，规定以"元"为单位，定银元为国币，革除银两制度，停止各省自行制造银元，银元的铸造权收归中央政府，并严格规定了银元的重量、成色。当年，天津造币总厂就试制新版大清银币，次年正式制造大清银币，面值为一元、五角、二角、一角四种，从此进入银元流通的阶段。

纸币

清咸丰三年（1853年），清政府为解决财政危机，发行了户部官票和大清宝钞两种纸币。"户部官票""大清宝钞"合称为"钞票"，也是"钞票"一词的起源。"钞票"与铜钱、铜元、白银并行流通，一度成为主要货币。此外，清代非官方金融机构或个人也印发私钞。

户部官票

户部官票又叫"银票"，票面写"户部官票"，对银作价，以银两为单位，有一两、三两、五两、

Coin of the Qing Dynasty and an official version the year followed. The coins were in denominations of 1 *Yuan*, 5 *Jiao*, 2 *Jiao*, and 1 *Jiao*, and from then on the nation entered an era of silver coin circulation.

Paper Money

In 1853, in order to address financial crisis, the Qing government issued *Hubu Guanpiao* and *Daqing Baochao*, two kinds of banknotes, which were together called as *Chaopiao*. It is also the origin of the Chinese word *Chaopiao* (paper currency). *Chaopiao* was circulated with the copper money, copper coin and the silver currency at the same time, and once became the main currency of that time. In addition, the unofficial financial institutions and the individuals also issued private banknotes.

Hubu Guanpiao

The *Hubu Guanpiao* was also called as *Yinpiao*, with characters "*Hu Bu Guan Piao*" written in the front, based on the price of silver, and used the *Liang* as the unit, including five nominal values of 1 *Liang*, 3 *Liang*, 5 *Liang*, 10 *Liang*, and 50 *Liang*. It was printed in rectangle and with the name of the banknote written in Han and Man languages in the upper corner. The nominal value was printed

• 户部官票五十两（清）
Hubu Guanpiao of the Nominal Value of 50 *Liang* (Qing Dynasty, 1616-1911)

十两、五十两五种面额。其形制为竖长型，额书满汉文票名，中标面额，左侧为发行时间，右侧为字号，下为赏格，用白色苔笺纸和高丽纸两种纸，加入靛蓝彩印制而成，先在京都发行，后在全国推行。户部官票行用不到十年，就因贬值而停用。

in the middle; the issuing time was on the left and the name of the institution was on the right. The reward was at the below. It was printed by white *Taijian* paper and *Gaoli* paper, added indigo blue pigment. The *Hubu Guanpiao* was firstly issued in Beijing, and then was promoted throughout the country. It was banned after circulating no more than ten years, because of the depreciation.

Daqing Baochao

Daqing Baochao is called *Baochao* for short, or *Qianpiao*, of which the unit is official copper coin, including nine nominal values of 250 *Wen*, 500 *Wen*, 1,000 *Wen*, 1,500 *Wen*, 2,000 *Wen*, 5,000 *Wen*, 10,000 *Wen*, 50,000 *Wen*, and 100,000 *Wen*. The name, nominal value, name of the institution and the issue time are printed on the top; and the circulation precautions are printed on the bottom.

Later on, the banknote was depreciated and disappeared in circulation sector, since the Qing government issued it massively in order to cover the military and fiscal expenditure.

Private Banknotes

Private banknotes refer to the paper currency issued by individuals or unofficial financial institutions such as private banks (named *Qianzhuang*,

大清宝钞

大清宝钞简称"宝钞",也称"钱票",以制钱为单位,有二百五十文、五百文、一千文、一千五百文、两千文、五千文、十千文、五十千文、百千文九种面额。额书钞名,中标面额、字号及发行时间,下为流通注意事项性质的文字。

后来,清政府为应付军事财政开支,大量发行宝钞,致使宝钞币值大跌,终因贬值而退出流通领域。

私钞

私钞是由民间的钱庄、票号、银号等非官方金融机构或个人发行的各种纸币。私钞又叫"民间票帖",是一种信用纸币,能在一定的地区和范围内流通。

- 大清宝钞百千文(清)
  Daqing Baochao of the Nominal Value of 100,000 *Wen* (Qing Dynasty, 1616-1911)

Piaohao or *Yinhao*) in ancient China. Private banknotes are also called "folk bill", a kind of credit note which circulated in certain areas and sectors.

Private banknotes had gained popularity in the Qianlong Period (1736-1795), which originated in inland towns and spread throughout provinces in China. There were rich contents on the notes including folk allusions, blessing words, the truth in life, etc. The private banknotes also came into several categories called *Yinpiao*, *Qianpiao*, *Yinyuanpiao* (special for civil dollar

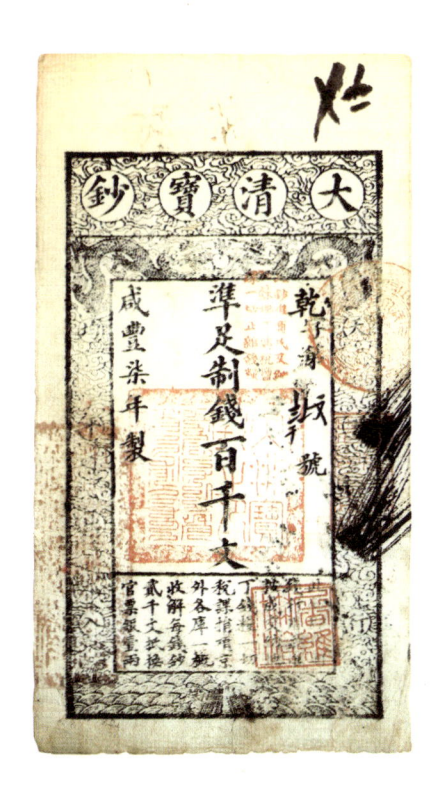

私钞在乾隆年间已经流行，最初大多发行于内地乡镇，后遍及各省，内容十分丰富，多反映民间的典故、吉语、为人、处事等，有银票、钱票、银元票、铜元票等多种。

清中末期，私钞流通盛行，印制也比较普遍。私钞有一定的使用期限，到期后私钞和钞版一并销毁。

清道光年间，国内银贵钱贱，印钞呼声渐起，加之其后太平军起义，咸丰皇帝不得不下令户部制印纸币。

exchange), *Tongyuanpiao* (special for copper coin exchange), etc.

In the end of the Qing Dynasty, circulation of the private notes and their printing enjoyed prevalence. Private banknotes had certain period of use, with the burning of both notes and printing mold at the end of the period.

In the Daoguang Period, silver appreciated relative to copper coins, leading to the demand for printing notes. Moreover, the Taiping Rebellion also prompted the Empire Xianfeng to issue official paper notes, with the Ministry of Revenue charged with the printing work.

清末银行发行的纸币
Banknotes Issued in the Late Qing Dynasty

清末民初，清政府成立了六家著名的银行，这些银行均发行过纸币。

In the late Qing Dynasty, the government set up six famous banks which all had issued banknotes.

中国通商银行

光绪二十三年（1897年）在上海设立，是中国近代第一家银行。中国通商银行成立以后，先后共发行过8个版次的钞票，钞票发行期长达38年之久，是中国近代史上发行钞票历史最长的商业银行。

光绪二十四年（1898年），中国通商银行开始发行横式银两票、银元票两种银行兑换券。银两票有一两、五两、十两、五十两、一百两五种面值，在北京、上海两地发行流通。银元票有一元、五元、十元、五十元、一百元五种面额，在北京、上海、广州三地行用。

- **中国通商银行发行的十两面值银两票（清）**

  银两票正面中间篆书"中国通商银行"，下为面值，背面为英文行名、面值等。

  Yinliangpiao of the Nominal Value of 10 *Liang* Issued by Imperial Bank of China (Qing Dynasty, 1616-1911)

  In the center of the banknote, the "中国通商银行" (Imperial Bank of China) is printed, below which is the nominal value. In the back, the name of the bank and its value is printed in English.

Imperial Bank of China

In 1897, the Imperial Bank of China was set up in Shanghai, which was the first bank in the Chinese modern history. Since its establishment, it issued eight versions of banknotes successively for 38 years, which was the commercial bank with the longest banknote's issue history in China.

In 1898, the Imperial Bank of China started to issue two exchange certificates, the *Yinliangpiao* of horizontal version and *Yinyuanpiao*. The former one had five nominal values of 1 *Liang*, 5 *Liang*, 10 *Liang*, 50 *Liang*, and 100 *Liang*, which circulated in Beijing and Shanghai. The latter one had five nominal values of 1 *Yuan*, 5 *Yuan*, 10 *Yuan*, 50 *Yuan*, and 100 *Yuan*, which was used in Beijing, Shanghai and Guangzhou.

户部银行、大清银行

光绪三十一年（1905年），清政府在北京设立户部银行，发行银两、银元、制钱票三种纸币。其中，银两票有28种，从一两至一千两，银元票有一元、五元、十元三种，制钱票的面值也大小不同。此外，又开办阜通钱号，设立东、西、南、北四号，专营门市兑换业务，发行制钱票。

光绪三十四年（1908年）改户部银行为大清银行，发行大清银行钞票，正式确立纸币发行制度。宣统二年（1910年）度支部颁布了《厘订国币则例》，规定纸币兑换券由大清银行发行，称为"大清银行兑换券"。大清银行发行的银两票，根据各地区的差异，有不同的称呼。如北京的银两票称为"库平足银"。银元票的形制有大有小。还发行有一种需要填写发行的特字票。

大清银行成立的当年，就停止各通商口岸外国租借外钞的流通。还设计印制了摄政王载沣头像的一元、五元、十元和一百元兑换券，计划统一纸币，但还没来得及实施，清政府就被推翻了。

Bank of Ministry of Revenue, Bank of Qing Dynasty

In 1905, the Qing government established the Bank of Ministry of Revenue in Beijing, issuing three kinds of banknotes, *Yinliang*, *Yinyuan*, and *Yinpiao*. *Yinliang* has 28 nominal values, ranging from 1 *Liang* to 1000 *Liang*; *Yinyuan* has 3 nominal values, which are 1 *Yuan*, 5 *Yuan*, and 10 *Yuan*; *Yinpiao* also has different nominal values. And the government opened Futong Money Shop with four branches in East, West, South, and North, specializing in money exchange and banknote issuing.

In 1908, the Bank of Ministry of Revenue was changed into Bank of the Qing Dynasty, issuing the banknote of the Qing Dynasty, which officially established the paper currency issue system. In 1910, the Ministry of Treasure proclaimed the "Regualtion of National Currency", which determined the exchange certificate only can be issued by the Bank of the Qing Dynasty, called as "exchange certificate of Bank of the Qing Dynasty". The *Yinliangpiao* issued by Bank of the Qing Dynasty varied in names according to the different areas. For instance, the *Yinliangpiao* in Beijing was called *Kuping Zuyin*. The form of *Yinyuanpiao* varied in the size. There was another *Tezipiao* issued, which needed to be filled in by the specific information.

In the first year of the establishment of Bank of the Qing Dynasty, the government stopped the circulation within the foreign leases in every open port, and designed the exchange certificate with the portrait of the Regent Zaifeng with the values of 1 *Yuan*, 5 *Yuan*, 10 *Yuan*, and 100 *Yuan* to unify the currency. But it was never carried out, as the Qing government was overthrown later.

华商上海信成银行

光绪三十二年（1906年），由无锡人周舜卿在上海创办，是中国第一家储蓄银行。于光绪三十三年（1907年）发行一元、五元、十元等面值银元票，票面左侧印有银行大楼图案，右侧印有商部尚书镇国将军载振像。光绪三十四年（1908年）又发行银两票，与银元票同时流通。

Huashang Shanghai Xincheng Bank

In 1906, the Huashang Shanghai Xincheng Bank was set up by Zhou Shunqing from Wuxi, in Shanghai, which was the first saving bank in China. In 1907, it issued the *Yinyuanpiao* with the nominal values of 1 *Yuan*, 5 *Yuan*, and 10 *Yuan*. On the left of the banknote, it was printed the bank's building; on the right, it was printed the portrait of the *Zhengguo* General, Zaizhen. In 1908, it issued *Yinliangpiao*, which could circulate with *Yinyuanpiao*.

- 华商上海信成银行发行的十元面值银元票（清）

Yinyuanpiao of the Nominal Value of 10 *Yuan* Issued by Huashang Shanghai Xincheng Bank (Qing Dynasty, 1616-1911)

交通银行

光绪三十三年（1907年）成立，为官商合办，商股六成。从宣统元年（1909年）起，发行第一版银两票，有一两、五两、十两、五十两四种，票面上印有地名济南；银元票有一元、五元、十元三种，票面上印有北京、南京、天津、上海、汉口、营口、张家口、济南、开封、广东等地名。此外，还发行有五角、十角、五十角、一百角四种小洋票，票面上印有地名营口。

Bank of Communications

In 1907, the Bank of Communications was established by politicians and businessmen, with the commercial shares of 60%. Since 1909, it issued first version of *Yinliangpiao* with the nominal values of 1 *Liang*, 5 *Liang*, 10 *Liang*, and 50 *Liang*. The location name Jinan is printed in the front; *Yinyuanpiao* has three nominal values of 1 *Yuan*, 5 *Yuan*, and 10 *Yuan*, with the location names of Beijing, Nanjing, Tianjin, Shanghai, Hankou, Yingkou, Zhangjiakou, Jinan, Kaifeng, and Guangdong. Besides, it issued small Yangpiao with the values of 5 *Jiao*, 10 *Jiao*, 50 *Jiao*, and 100 *Jiao*, with the location name Yingkou printed in front.

浙江兴业银行

光绪三十三年（1907年）成立，是中国第一家商办商业银行。从成立之日起，发行第一版银元票，面值有一元、五元、十元三种，票面图案为银行和火车。光绪三十四年（1908年），发行第二版铜元票，竖式，面值一百枚（当十铜元）。宣统元年（1909年），发行第三版银元票，有一元、五元、十元三种。其中一元券正面图案是王阳明像，配有明代"大明通行宝钞"图案；五元券正面图案为管仲像，配以先秦布币图案；十元券正面图案是齐太公像，配有先秦刀币图案。各券背面均统一为"公鸡报晓"图案。

Industrial Bank of Zhejiang

In 1907, the Industrial Bank of Zhejiang was set up and was the first commercial bank owned by businessmen. From the day it established, it issued the first version of *Yinyuanpiao*, with the values of 1 *Yuan*, 5 *Yuan*, and 10 *Yuan*, with the patterns of bank and train. In 1908, it issued the second version of *Tongyuanpiao*, in vertical format, with the value of 100 *Mei* (equals to 10 copper coins). In 1909, it issued the third version of *Yinyuanpiao*, with the values of 1 *Yuan*, 5 *Yuan* and 10 *Yuan*. And the 1 *Yuan* banknote is with the portrait of Wang Yangming printed in front, and matching the pattern of "*Daming Tongxing Baochao*" of the Ming Dynasty; 5 *Yuan* banknote is with the portrait of Guan Zhong printed in front, and matching the pattern of the *Bu* coin of the pre-Qin Period; 10 *Yuan* banknote is with the portrait of Qi Taigong printed in front, and matching the pattern of the knife-shaped coin of the pre-Qin Period. All of these banknotes have a pattern of "Herald the Break of Day the Rooster" printed at back.

四明银行

光绪三十四年（1908年）在上海成立。从宣统元年（1909年）起，四明银行发行第一版银元票，面值有一元、二元、五元、十元四种。票面印有"上海四明银行"行名，主景图为四明山，印有地名上海，也有用木戳加盖的宁波、温州、处州、镇江等地名，由上海华商集成图书公司印造。同年，还发行由上海商务印书馆印制的第二版银元票，面值有一元、五元、十元三种。

Siming Bank

In 1908, Siming Bank was established in Shanghai. From 1909, it issued the first version of *Yinyuanpiao*, with the values of 1 *Yuan*, 2 *Yuan*, 5 *Yuan*, and 10 *Yuan*. The name of the bank "上海四明银行" is printed in the front. The banknote is printed with the main landscape of Siming Mountain. And the location name, Shanghai is printed too; and some other places are stamped by the wooden seals, like Ningbo, Wenzhou, Chuzhou, Zhenjiang, etc. It was printed by the Shanghai Huashang jicheng Book Company. In the same year, it issued the second version of *Yinyuanpiao*, with the values of 1 *Yuan*, 5 *Yuan* and 10 *Yuan*.